The Friends and Foes of Jesus

Discover How People in the New Testament React to God's Good News

Peter DeHaan, PhD

ISBNs:

    978-1-948082-13-6 (e-book)
    978-1-948082-12-9 (paperback)
    978-1-948082-21-1 (hardcover)

Published by Spiritually Speaking Publishing

Credits:

    Developmental editor: Cathy Rueter
    Copy editor/proofreader: Robyn Mulder
    Cover design: Cassia Friello
    Author photo: Chele Reagh, PippinReaghDesign

To Dan DeHaan

Table of Contents

Other Books by Peter DeHaan

The Bible Bios series:

- *Women of the Bible: The Victorious, the Victims, the Virtuous, and the Vicious*

The Dear Theophilus series:

- *Dear Theophilus: A 40-Day Devotional Exploring the Life of Jesus through the Gospel of Luke*
- *Dear Theophilus, Acts: 40 Devotional Insights for Today's Church*
- *Dear Theophilus, Isaiah: 40 Prophetic Insights about Jesus, Justice, and Gentiles*
- *Dear Theophilus, Minor Prophets: 40 Prophetic Teachings about Unfaithfulness, Punishment, and Hope*
- *Dear Theophilus, Job: 40 Insights About Moving from Despair to Deliverance*

The 52 Churches series:

- *52 Churches: A Yearlong Journey Encountering God, His Church, and Our Common Faith*
- *The 52 Churches Workbook: Become a Church that Matters*
- *More Than 52 Churches: The Journey Continues*
- *The More Than 52 Churches Workbook: Pursue Christian Community and Grow in Our Faith*

Other books:

- *Woodpecker Wars: Celebrating the Spirituality of Everyday Life*
- *95 Tweets: Celebrating Martin Luther in the 21st Century*
- *How Big is Your Tent? A Call for Christian Unity, Tolerance, and Love*

Be the first to find out about Peter's new books and receive monthly updates when you sign up at www.PeterDeHaan.com/updates.

Jesus

I f you could sum up the Bible in one word, what would it be? This isn't a trick question. For a hint, look at the title of this chapter. The one word I choose to sum up the Bible is *Jesus*.

Though the Old Testament of the Bible focuses on God's people and their relationship with him, it also looks forward to a coming savior. It anticipates Jesus. From our perspective today, Jesus is the point of the Old Testament. Seriously.

The New Testament of the Bible, of course, is all about Jesus. It starts by covering his life from the perspectives of four biographers: Matthew, Mark, Luke, and John. Then it moves into the work of Jesus's followers as they share the good news of Jesus with as many people as they can.

Just as today, some people of the New Testament decide to follow him, and others don't. Everyone moves toward one of these two conclusions. In the end, they're either for him or against him. They're either *friend* or *foe*.

Not only is Jesus the central figure in the Bible, many say he's the central figure in all of history. I am one of those people.

Jesus is amazing. I talk about him in the present tense because he is a present reality in my life. Though many people think that Jesus *was*, to me he *is*. Embracing him in the present brings him closer and makes him more accessible. In fact, when I write about the people in the Bible, I often use present tense for the same reason: to bring them closer and make them more accessible.

I do this to understand Jesus better. What's your understanding of him?

Do you think of Jesus as meek and mild or bold and brash? Is Jesus easygoing or intense? Does he draw people in with his love or make them cringe with his criticism? Does Jesus produce unity or cause division?

Don't think about this too hard. The answer is yes! Yes, to all the above.

Wherever Jesus goes, whatever he does, and whatever he says provokes a reaction. People are either drawn to him or repelled. They either love him or hate him. Just as it was true 2,000 years ago, it is true today.

Consider the people of the New Testament. Some are for Jesus and others are against him. Some are willing to die for him and others want to silence him forever.

Join me as we explore these friends and foes of Jesus. May their lives encourage us and challenge us. May our search bring us closer to Jesus and deepen our relationship with him.

Let's move from Jesus as our friend to Jesus as our best friend forever—our BFF—one who will never let us down, never forget us, and never leave us. Jesus can be the ultimate BFF. All we need to do is follow him and be his disciple.

How do you view Jesus? Does the idea of Jesus being our BFF shock you or encourage you?

[Discover more about Jesus in the New Testament of the Bible. Learn more about Jesus's love for us in John 13:34–35, about friendship in Proverbs 18:24, and about God's forever promise in Deuteronomy 31:6 and Hebrews 13:5.]

Part 1:

The Beginning

For this first section of *The Friends and Foes of Jesus*, we'll look at the events of Jesus's birth. The people surrounding his arrival react in different ways. Some are astounded and amazed, often offering affirmation of Jesus and praise to God. But one person—Herod—is dismayed. He doesn't view Jesus's arrival as good news at all. Herod sees Jesus as a threat.

But we're getting ahead of ourselves. Before Jesus, we need John the Baptist. We'll start our story with him and his beginning. Just as John prepares the way for Jesus's ministry, he also precedes Jesus in birth.

Throughout these stories about John the Baptist and Jesus, we see supernatural events that inspire awe and heighten our expectations of what is to come. Embrace the people in this section for their testimony of Jesus and the new work that God is beginning.

Our first entry is Zechariah. Did you know there are twenty-two people in the Bible named Zechariah? We'll refer to this one as Zechariah (22). Through the rest of this book, whenever we encounter a duplicate name, we'll add a number at the end. You can learn more about this in Bonus Content 1, "Duplicate Names."

Zechariah (22)

Elderly Zechariah and his wife, Elizabeth, have no kids. They're past their childbearing years. From a human perspective, having a baby is impossible, yet they pray for one anyway.

They're a righteous pair, Zechariah and Elizabeth. They obey all God's commands and follow his rules—all of them. They're descendants of Aaron. In addition, Zechariah works for God. He's a priest.

Did you catch that?

They're good people. They're obedient and do the right things. They have the ideal heritage, and Zechariah lives to serve God.

For all this devotion, shouldn't God bless them with the child they yearn for? Yet each year passes and no baby. Still they continue to pray for a kid.

Then things change.

One day the angel Gabriel shows up at the temple, right when Zechariah's supposed to burn the incense for church. How inconvenient. The people are waiting for Zechariah to kick off their religious ceremony. Couldn't Gabriel have come a few minutes later?

But Gabriel has good news. God will soon answer Zechariah and Elizabeth's years of prayers. They'll finally have a baby, a son. "Name him John."

And how does Zechariah respond? He says, "Really? Elizabeth and I are too old."

Frankly, I'd say that too.

Gabriel takes this as a sign of unbelief. To make his point, he removes Zechariah's ability to talk, which makes it difficult for the poor guy to lead worship. He gestures to let the people know he has seen a vision from God. Astonishing.

When his stint in the temple is over, Zechariah goes home, still mute. Take time to imagine what happens when he arrives, what he communicates through gestures, and most importantly, what happens next. Elizabeth gets pregnant. God is good.

How long will we wait for God to answer our prayers and give us what we yearn for? Do we have faith to believe in the improbable? The impossible?

[Discover more about Zechariah in Luke 1:5–25. See Bonus Content 1, "Duplicate Names" for more info about other men in the Bible named Zechariah.]

Elizabeth

Childless, Elizabeth and her husband, Zechariah, are getting old. Seriously old. Their chance to have kids is slim. Still, they pray for the improbable. Despite not receiving what they yearn for, their faith remains strong. They're an upright couple who honor God.

One day an angel shows up at her husband's work. This messenger from God promises Zechariah that he and Elizabeth will finally have a baby. A son, but not just any son—a special one. They must set him apart for service to God. The Holy Spirit will empower him. Then their child will spark a nationwide revival.

They are to name him John.

Elizabeth does indeed get pregnant. In her sixth month, Mary—who is also expecting—comes for a visit. Inside Elizabeth, baby John jumps for joy at the sound of Mary's voice. Then the Holy Spirit comes upon Elizabeth and she prophesies, blessing Mary and her unborn baby.

After John is born, Elizabeth and Zechariah's friends and family gather to celebrate. They praise God and share in Elizabeth's joy at finally having a baby. God has taken away Elizabeth's shame over her childless condition.

Elizabeth and Zechariah prayed for a child even when it no longer made sense, when their bodies were too old to cooperate—at least from a human perspective. Yet they persevered in faith.

God answered their prayers by giving them a son named John, who will later become John the Baptist. He does, indeed, spark a national revival that features repentance and points the way to Jesus.

What if Elizabeth and Zechariah had stopped believing and ceased their prayers? John wouldn't have been born. Then who would have opened the door for Jesus to change the world?

Are we willing to pray for the impossible? Will we patiently wait for God's answer?

[Discover more about Elizabeth in Luke 1:5–60.]

John (1) the Baptist

The angel Gabriel says John won't be just any kid, but a special one. People will celebrate his birth. John's parents must set him apart for service to God. The Holy Spirit will empower him, and he'll spark a nationwide revival. In the mold of Elijah, he'll do amazing things and pave the way for the Savior the Old Testament prophets wrote about. God's people have waited for this for centuries.

When John the Baptist begins his ministry, he proclaims, "The kingdom of heaven is near." He preaches repentance and baptizes people who want to show that they're sorry for the wrong things they've done. They desire to make a U-turn with their life.

Even though Jesus is perfect and doesn't need to repent, he insists John baptize him. Afterward the Holy Spirit comes upon Jesus and a voice booms from heaven, proclaiming him as God's son.

Though the main part of John's work—preparing the way for Jesus—is over, John continues his ministry. One of the things he does proves fatal. He criticizes Herod for marrying his brother's wife. Infuriated, Herod arrests John and throws him in jail. Despite this, Herod fears John, and is puzzled by what he says, so Herod protects him.

Yet Herod's wife, Herodias, holds a grudge against John. She looks for an opportunity to silence him for good.

When Herod throws a lavish birthday party for himself, Herodias has her chance. Her daughter dances at the party and impresses everyone. Herod promises to give her anything she wants. At her mother's prompting, she asks for the head of John the Baptist, served up on a silver tray.

Though he doesn't want to do this, Herod won't back down in front of his guests. He orders the execution of John.

John faithfully does what God tells him to do. He prepares the way for Jesus. And the people in power kill him for it.

If serving God would result in our execution, would we still obey him?

[Discover more about John the Baptist in Matthew 3:1–17, Mark 6:14–29, and Luke 1:11–17, 57–66.]

Mary (1)

Now, let's look back to before John the Baptist was born.

An angel visits Mary, a young virgin, engaged but not married. The angel celebrates her as one highly favored by God. Mary wonders about the angel's shocking greeting. He further stuns her by saying she'll get pregnant, and her child will grow up to save her people.

"How?" Mary asks. "I'm a virgin."

The angel explains that the Holy Spirit will supernaturally impregnate her.

Mary accepts the angel's words without arguing. She trusts God.

When Joseph, her fiancé, finds out she's with child, he plans to break their engagement, but an angel visits him, too, and tells him not to. They get married but remain celibate until after Mary's miracle baby is born.

However, before this happens, Mary and Joseph must travel to Bethlehem for a mandatory census. Unable to find a place to stay, they hunker down in a barn. There, among the filth of livestock, Jesus is born.

This is no ordinary birth: angels cheer, shepherds bow down, and later magi offer lavish gifts. Eight days later, at Jesus's consecration ceremony, people say amazing things about him. First Simeon and then Anna. Twelve years later, Jesus stuns his parents when they find him at the temple in deep discussion with the religious leaders.

At age thirty Jesus starts his ministry. Three years later, during his execution, Jesus makes sure Mary will be cared for. The last we hear of her is at a gathering of Jesus's followers after he rises from the dead and returns to heaven.

We commend Mary for her pious acceptance of God's assignment. The townspeople, however, likely condemn her for getting pregnant before she and Joseph say, "I do." Who would believe her claim that "God did it?" She likely forever carries the stigma as the girl who got pregnant before she was married.

Sometimes we must suffer for following God. Are we willing to bear a lifetime of humiliation to obey his plan for us?

[Discover more about Mary in Matthew 1:18–2:11, Luke 1:26–38, Luke 2:1–51, and Acts 1:14.]

Joseph (4)

Joseph's excited. He's engaged. Mary's the perfect girl for him. She's chaste and devout. Her deep faith matches his own.

Then everything falls apart.

Joseph hears that his fiancée, the one he knew as pure, is pregnant. He must end their engagement, but, being a good man, he doesn't want to make life any harder for her. He plans a private breakup.

But before he acts, God sends an angel to him in a dream. The angel says, "Don't dump her. Proceed as planned. Her pregnancy is not of human origin but from the Holy Spirit. This divine-human conception will produce a child who will save the people from their sins. Name him Jesus."

That's a lot to take in.

Joseph does as the angel instructs. He marries Mary, but they don't consummate their relationship until after Jesus is born. Then, an angel again comes to Joseph in a dream, "Quick! Leave! Herod's trying to kill your baby. Hightail it to Egypt." Again, Joseph obeys.

Later, in Egypt, an angel again comes to Joseph in a dream. "Herod's dead. It's safe to return to Israel." A third time Joseph obeys God's instructions. They settle in Nazareth.

Fast-forward twelve years. Joseph and Mary head to Jerusalem for the Passover. On their trip home, things get hairy. After one day of travel, they discover Jesus isn't part of the caravan. Joseph and Mary rush back to Jerusalem to find their son. Their worry is more intense than what other parents would feel. They lost the Son of God.

Three days later, they find him in the temple courts, talking theology with the Jewish teachers. When they scold him for causing them worry, Jesus says, "Didn't you know I'd be in Papa's house?"

Joseph and Mary don't get it. I can't blame them. I wouldn't either.

Regardless, Joseph obeys God at each turn, and he does so without hesitation.

When God tells us to do something crazy, how willing are we to obey?

[Discover more about Joseph in Matthew 1:18–25, Matthew 2:13–23, and Luke 2:1–40.]

King Herod (1)

After the birth of Jesus, King Herod's in a tizzy. Here's why.

Visitors from the Far East, magi, have shown up unannounced. They're searching for a new king who has been born, the king of the Jews. They've seen his star in the sky and have come to worship him.

This is news to Herod.

He knows nothing about a star or a baby who will be king. He is the king.

This news threatens his reign and his power. He must squash this menace child, lest the baby seize his throne.

Yet Herod plays it cool with the magi. "Go and find the baby," he says, "and then update me, so I can worship him too."

Yet the magi don't report back to Herod. An angel warns them of his deception. By the time Herod realizes this, the magi have already left the country.

Herod is furious.

He intended to kill baby Jesus. But since he doesn't know which baby Jesus is, he gives orders to kill all the baby boys in Bethlehem. Now many babies die instead of just one.

What anguish this causes the families of these babies. Their young sons, innocent and having done nothing wrong, are executed by a power-hungry king who wants to ensure his ongoing rule.

What Herod doesn't know is that his heinous scheme is too late. Before he gives the order, Joseph already whisked Mary and Jesus away and fled into Egypt. There, they are safe from Herod's reach.

Herod has immense power and is corrupted by it. To hold onto his reign as king, he slaughters many innocent babies. But God is more powerful than this evil king and thwarts his plan.

We all have a degree of power. Do we use the power we have for good or for evil? Do we help others or serve ourselves?

[Discover more about King Herod in Mathew 2:1–23.]

The Magi

The story of the magi intersects with King Herod (1). We've already covered this from Herod's point of view. Now we'll look at it from the magi's perspective. But first, know that the Bible doesn't say there are three of them, only that they give three gifts: gold, frankincense, and myrrh.

The magi, aka wise men, travel from the East searching for a baby born to be king of the Jews. They've come to worship him.

They make their journey, based on a new star they spot in the sky, following it west until they reach Jerusalem. They assume he'll be born to Herod in the palace. After all, this baby will be king.

This is news to Herod—bad news. A baby who could one day become king threatens Herod's rule. He must squash this danger, but he doesn't let the magi know his plans. He pretends he wants to worship the baby king too. He feigns interest and requests they report their findings back to him. Then, based on a tip from the religious leaders who know what the Scriptures say about the coming Messiah, Herod sends the magi to Bethlehem.

They continue their journey, using the star to home in on their destination. It stops over Bethlehem where Jesus and his parents are. The magi enter the place and bow down to Jesus in reverent worship. Then they give him the gifts they brought, gifts of gold, frankincense, and myrrh.

Having finished their mission, they're ready to return home, but an angel warns them in a dream to not report their findings to Herod. So they sneak out of town and take a different route home. They're long gone—and so are Mary, Joseph, and Jesus—before Herod realizes he was duped.

God sent the magi a message in a dream and they obeyed, thereby saving Jesus.

Does God ever communicate to us in dreams? How do we react when he does?

[Discover more about the magi in Matthew 2:1–16.]

Simeon (2)

Simeon's a good guy. He's serious about following God and obeying all the religious rules. He believes the prophecies that say God will send someone to save them. Even though his people have waited for centuries, Simeon lives in expectation that God will rescue them as he promised long ago.

The Holy Spirit reveals to Simeon that this coming savior will arrive in his lifetime. God promises Simeon that he will see Jesus with his own eyes.

Throughout the centuries, people lived their whole lives with faith-filled expectation that they would see God's promised Messiah, only to die before they realized their hope. Yet, God promises that Simeon will witness this firsthand. But God doesn't say when.

Then one day the Holy Spirit prompts Simeon to go to the temple courts. Is today the day? He goes. He waits. His pulse no doubt quickens as he looks around, scanning the people milling about. Which one is the Messiah?

Then baby Jesus arrives with his parents. They come to fulfill the religious rituals commanded long ago by Moses. Simeon walks up. He takes baby Jesus in his arms and praises God. What must Jesus's parents think?

Simeon affirms Jesus as the promised Savior for Israel—and for the entire world. His words shock Joseph and Mary. Then Simeon blesses them and prophesies.

Now, having seen Jesus firsthand, Simeon's life is complete. He gives it over to God, knowing that he can now die in peace, with the knowledge that Jesus has arrived.

A lifetime of anticipation has now been fulfilled for Simeon. But what if he had ignored the Holy Spirit's nudge and stayed home that day?

How well do we do at listening to the Holy Spirit and obeying his prompting?

[Discover more about Simeon in Luke 2:25–35.]

Anna

First there is Simeon and then Anna.

Anna is widowed after only seven years of marriage. A devout woman, she dedicates her life to God. Devoted to her creator, she spends as much time as possible in the temple. There she fasts, prays, and worships God. Luke calls her a prophet.

She is at least eighty-four years old—perhaps much older—when Mary and Joseph show up to consecrate their baby, Jesus. Anna sees them and walks over to the family. She recognizes baby Jesus as the savior the people have been expecting for centuries. She thanks God she's lived long enough to see what the prophets foretold. Then she shares her excitement with everyone nearby.

After a lifetime of devotion to God, Anna receives her reward by seeing Jesus—even though he's an infant and won't start his ministry for three decades. Yet this is enough for her. Now she knows God is fulfilling his long-ago promise to rescue his people. She has seen him.

How many other people were likewise as devout, but never got to see Jesus?

God calls us to focus on him, but we may not receive any reward for our loyalty during our lifetime. Will we be faithful anyway?

[Discover more about Anna in Luke 2:36–38.]

Part 2:

The Ministry of Jesus

For this section of *The Friends and Foes of Jesus*, we'll look at the work of Jesus. Some of the people we encounter are on his side. Others are against him. But for most of them, their interaction with Jesus changes their lives. Regardless, what we read about them can also change our lives and inform how we follow Jesus.

Simon (1)/Peter/Cephas

Simon, whom Jesus calls Peter (Cephas), is one of Jesus's twelve disciples. He's also part of Jesus's inner circle of three, along with James and John.

Peter often receives criticism and even ridicule for his behavior. He sometimes speaks before he thinks, his doubt causes him to sink when he tries to walk on water, and he denies even knowing Jesus. During Jesus's arrest, Peter whips out a sword and slashes at someone, but all he gets is an ear.

But let's not focus on these things. Let's look at the positive.

Peter is the only one of the twelve disciples who walks on water. Though his journey is short before his faith falters, remember that he's the only one to leave the safety of the boat. The other eleven don't even dare to try. Peter does, and his faith is rewarded.

Later when Jesus asks his disciples, "What do people say about me?" they give various answers. Then Jesus gets direct. "What do *you* say?"

Not surprisingly, Peter speaks first. He states with boldness, "You're the Christ, the son of the living God."

Jesus blesses Peter for his spot-on answer. This truth sets the foundation for Jesus's church.

After Jesus rises from the dead and returns to heaven, Peter emerges as the church's first leader—effectively the first Pope.

Then, Peter speaks on Pentecost under Holy Spirit power, and 3,000 people believe.

Later people lay the sick on the streets so that Peter's shadow might fall on them as he walks by. The Bible never says these folks are healed, but with their friends positioning them this way, there must be a good reason to do so.

In addition, Peter later writes two books of the New Testament: 1 Peter and 2 Peter.

Like all of us, Peter has his strengths and his weaknesses. May we seek to emulate the positive parts of Peter's example and avoid the negative.

Do we choose to focus on people's admirable traits or their faults?

[Discover more about Peter in Matthew 16:13–18, Acts 2:14–41, and Acts 5:15. Read Peter's two letters: 1 Peter and 2 Peter.]

Andrew

A ndrew, another of Jesus's disciples, is Peter's brother, presumably his younger brother. They're fishermen. When Jesus asks them to be his disciples, he tells them that going forward, they'll fish for people.

While the Bible talks about Peter a lot, Andrew receives only a few mentions. And when his name does occur, it's usually along with his brother. It seems Andrew is destined to be forever connected with his more outgoing sibling.

However, the Bible has two stories about Andrew.

Once, when a huge crowd (the Bible says 5,000 men, plus women and children) gathers to listen to Jesus, he wants to give them something to eat. Though he already knows what he's going to do, he uses this as a teaching moment for his disciples.

After Philip, another of the disciples, realizes they don't have enough money to buy food, Andrew offers a hopeful suggestion. He brings them a boy with five small loaves of bread and two tiny fish. It's not enough, but it's a start.

Yet with Jesus this is more than enough. He supernaturally multiplies this small amount of food, feeds everyone gathered, and has leftovers. Though Andrew's part in this miracle is small, he is the catalyst to make it happen.

Another time, some people from Greece want to meet Jesus. They approach Philip and ask for an introduction. What does Philip do? He tells Andrew. (It's interesting that Philip and Andrew appear together in both stories.) Together Philip and Andrew go tell Jesus about the people who want to see him. Though we don't know why Philip doesn't do this himself, we can surmise that he looks to Andrew as someone who can help make it happen. Even though we have no hint of Andrew being a leader among the twelve disciples, Philip must have looked up to him.

How do we react when we find ourselves in someone's shadow? What do we do when a friend asks for help?

[Discover more about Andrew in John 6:8–9 and John 12:20–22.]

James (1)

Just like Peter and Andrew, James and his brother, John, are disciples of Jesus. Since the Bible usually lists James first and John second, we can assume James is older. Peter, James, and John make up Jesus's inner circle.

Mark records an interesting nickname that Jesus gives the brothers. He calls them "the Sons of Thunder." This suggests the boys might be loud when they talk, perhaps like their dad.

Though once James and John ask Jesus if they can call down fire from heaven to destroy a Samaritan village who rejected them—Jesus says, "No"—the Bible doesn't give any other examples of brazen behavior by the boys. Yet calling them the Sons of Thunder suggests otherwise.

This might be a family characteristic, too, because James's mom does something bold for her boys. She goes to Jesus and asks him to honor her sons by letting them sit on Jesus's right and left when he rules his kingdom. Again, Jesus says, "No."

Like Andrew, whom the Bible usually mentions along with brother Peter, the same occurs for James, who's usually paired with brother John. Even though

James is part of Jesus's inner circle, he doesn't seem to play a vital role in Jesus's ministry or in the early church.

In the book of Acts, we read that King Herod (2) arrests some of Jesus's followers to harass them. This includes James, whom Herod executes. James becomes an early martyr of the church (after Stephen).

Though Jesus selects James to be his disciple and includes him in his inner circle of confidants, it seems James doesn't live up to the promise Jesus sees in him—or perhaps his premature death keeps him from reaching his potential.

We each have potential to serve God and help others. Do we live up to what God sees in us or fall short? Are we doing all we can today, in case we're not around tomorrow?

[Discover more about James in Matthew 20:20–24, Mark 3:17, Luke 9:52–55, and Acts 12:1–2.]

John (2), the Disciple

The fourth of Jesus's disciples that we'll cover is John (not to be confused with John the Baptist). John the disciple is the younger brother of James and is part of Jesus's inner circle, along with Peter and James.

However, John may have an even higher standing. Though John never mentions himself by name in his biography of Jesus, five times he refers to himself as the disciple whom Jesus loved. Consider that Jesus has many disciples and even more followers. He picks twelve of them to be *the* disciples and three of them to be in his inner circle, but John surpasses them all. He's the disciple Jesus loves.

Later, in the book of Acts, we see John in tandem with Peter telling others about Jesus, healing people, and getting arrested as a result. When they're released from jail, they visit the believers in Samaria and lay hands on them to receive the Holy Spirit.

After that we don't hear much more about John in the Bible's narrative, but he does write a lot. During the writing of his last book, Revelation, he's exiled on the island of Patmos.

John contributes much to the New Testament of the Bible. Only Paul and Luke write more. John pens one of the four biographies about Jesus in the Bible. It's called the Gospel of John or John for short. Many people cite this biography of Jesus as their favorite for its poetic language and unique content.

John also writes three letters, called 1 John, 2 John, and 3 John. His fifth book is an epic vision of the future, called Revelation. Together these five books make up about 20 percent of the content in the New Testament.

We may want to do amazing things for Jesus just like John, but are we willing to suffer exile like he did?

[Discover more about John in John 21:20–24, Acts 4:1–22, Acts 8:14–17, and Revelation 1:9. Explore the five books of the Bible that John wrote: John, 1 John, 2 John, 3 John, and Revelation.]

Philip (1)

The day after Jesus calls Peter and Andrew to follow him, Jesus sees Philip and tells him to "follow me." Then Philip goes and finds his buddy, Nathanael, and tells him about Jesus.

The next time we see Philip is at the miracle feeding of 5,000 men (plus women and children), and then he's in the story about the Greeks who want to see Jesus. We already covered these when we talked about Andrew.

Later Jesus says, "I'm the way, the truth, and the life. No one can come to Papa except through me. If you know me, you know my father."

To this Philip replies, "Show us the father, and that'll be good enough."

Jesus scolds Philip. "After all this time, you still don't know me? If you see me, you've seen Papa."

Philip may wish he hadn't opened his mouth. His words just proved that he doesn't know Jesus as well as he thought he did. Ouch!

How well do we know Jesus? What would be Jesus's answer to that question?

[Discover more about Philp in John 1:43–46, John 6:5–7, John 12:20–22, and John 14:6–11.]

Thomas (Didymus)

The sixth of Jesus's disciples is Thomas, also known as Didymus. Though Matthew, Mark, and Luke only mention Thomas once, and that's in their list of Jesus's disciples, John gives us more insight into his character. John shares three stories about Thomas.

First, as Jesus wraps up his time on earth, before his execution, he tells his disciples what to expect. After encouraging them to believe in God and in him, he says that Papa's house has many rooms. "I'll go there and get ready for you. Then I'll come back and get you, so we can hang out." Then Jesus adds, "You know the way there."

Thomas is confused and reacts as I imagine I would. He wants more info. "We don't know where you're going, so how can we know how to get there?"

Jesus responds with a familiar passage. "I'm the way, the truth, and the life. To get to Papa, you must go through me." Frankly this explanation wouldn't have helped me too much. We don't know if Thomas gets it or not, but he says nothing more.

The second story is what we most know about Thomas. It's the source of the phrase *doubting Thomas*.

When Jesus rises from the dead and first appears to his disciples, Thomas isn't there. When his buddies insist Jesus is alive, Thomas doesn't believe them. He demands proof. That sounds reasonable.

Third, a week later, the disciples hunker behind locked doors, and Jesus appears in the room. He goes to Thomas and shows him the nail scars in his hand. He encourages Thomas to touch his side where the soldier's spear impaled him. "Stop doubting," Jesus says, "and believe."

Thomas does. "My Lord and my God!"

Jesus blesses Thomas because he sees and believes. But we're even more blessed because we haven't seen and believe anyway.

How should we deal with the struggle of faith versus doubt?

[Discover more about Thomas in John 14:3–7, John 20:24–29, and John 21:1–3.]

Matthew/Levi (5)

atthew is seventh on our list of Jesus's disciples, though he may be one of the earlier ones that Jesus calls. Mark and Luke both refer to him as Levi, the fifth person in the Bible with that name, Levi (5).

The one thing we know about Matthew is that he collects taxes. Often when the Bible mentions tax collectors it's part of the phrase "tax collectors and sinners." Though this doesn't imply that being a tax collector is a sinful job, it makes it clear that people don't think much of tax collectors. Nor do the Pharisees—a group of religious devotees who pursue righteous behavior with legalistic fervor. (Jesus often criticizes Pharisees for not seeing what God's doing.)

Jesus, while making a point that the people society looks down upon will have their place in heaven—ahead of the religious elite—uses the phrase "tax collectors and prostitutes." That's another disparaging pairing of two less-than-honorable professions. Last, in one of Jesus's parables, he lumps tax collectors in with thieves, evil people, and adulterers.

Matthew's occupation certainly carries a stigma. From a human standpoint we wouldn't want someone like Matthew on our team, but Jesus has a different perspective. He *wants* someone like Matthew on his squad. Jesus invites Matthew to be part of his posse.

When Jesus invites Matthew to "follow me," Matthew does so right away.

Then Jesus parties with Matthew and his friends—other tax collectors and "sinners." The religious leaders, of course, criticize Jesus for who he's hanging out with. But these people are exactly who Jesus wants to be with. By making Matthew part of his team he gives us a fresh perspective of who's in and who's out in his kingdom. Most people believe that Matthew later wrote a biography of Jesus, which we call the book of Matthew.

We all have a past. Do we let our past define us or do we accept God's mercy and move into something greater?

[Discover more about Matthew, also called Levi, in Matthew 9:9–13, Mark 2:13–17, and Luke 5:27–32. Read verses about tax collectors in Matthew 21:31–32 and Luke 7:34.]

Bartholomew, James (2) Son of Alphaeus, and Simon (2) the Zealot

For the next three disciples, we'll cover them together. You'll see why in a bit. They are Bartholomew, James son of Alphaeus, and Simon the Zealot.

These three disciples only appear four times in the Bible. Each time they're in a roster of the twelve disciples. Aside from being listed as one of the Twelve, they do nothing noteworthy that Matthew, Mark, Luke, or John feel they need to share—at least not explicitly.

However, right after Matthew shares the names of the twelve disciples, Jesus sends all twelve out on mission trips. He instructs them to tell other Jews that the kingdom of heaven is near. As they do this, they are to heal sick people, resurrect the dead, remove people's leprosy, and cast out demons. Whether we understand demon possession as a spiritual condition or as first century man's understanding of mental illness doesn't matter. What does matter is that the disciples deal with it.

It's one thing to tell other people about Jesus, but to also heal them is even more mind-boggling. Yet Jesus has prepared them to do both or he wouldn't have sent them. They know his message. And through his power they supernaturally heal people. This applies to all twelve disciples, including Bartholomew, James, and Simon.

They preach, and they heal.

Though the things this trio does—either good or bad—aren't detailed in the Bible, they do help advance Jesus's kingdom.

Will we be faithful to God's call even if we don't receive recognition for the work we do?

[Discover more about Bartholomew, James Son of Alphaeus, and Simon the Zealot in Matthew 10:2–4, Mark 3:16–20, Luke 6:14–16, and Acts 1:13.]

Thaddaeus and Judas (3) the Son of James (4)

Next we'll consider two more disciples in tandem. They're Thaddaeus and Judas, the son of James. What makes them unique is that they didn't make all four of the lists of disciples. Instead, they're each referred to twice—not four times like Bartholomew, James, Simon, and the rest of the group.

Matthew and Mark both mention Thaddaeus as one of the twelve disciples. However, Luke omits Thaddaeus in both his books (Luke and Acts). Instead he includes Judas, the son of James, who Matthew and Mark both omit.

Why the difference?

We're left to wonder why the Bible has this discrepancy. It could be that Mark got it wrong and Matthew copied him. (Some Bible scholars believe the book of Mark was written first, and Matthew based his on it.) Or it could be that Luke got the names wrong when he researched and wrote about Jesus and the early church.

Another possibility is that Thaddaeus starts out as a disciple but then leaves, with Judas, son of James, taking over.

A third explanation is that twelve isn't a literal number but figurative. It could be there are twelve disciples, perhaps thirteen, or maybe even more.

A fourth option is that Jesus's band of twelve is a dynamic group with people coming and going. Therefore, the roster changes over time.

Regardless, the Bible says that both Thaddaeus and Judas, son of James, are disciples. Let's celebrate them as such.

How do we react when our name is omitted from a list of people serving Jesus or someone else's name is inserted for the work we did?

[Discover more about Thaddaeus in Matthew 10:3 and Mark 3:18. Read about Judas the Son of James in Luke 6:16, and Acts 1:13.]

Judas (1) Iscariot

L ast on our list of twelve disciples is the notorious one. His name is Judas, often called Judas Iscariot. His father is Simon (7) Iscariot.

We know Judas for his betrayal of Jesus. Some passages in the Bible call him a traitor. That's a more fitting term. He agrees to turn on Jesus and help the religious authorities arrest him. He does this for thirty pieces of silver. Money matters more to him than loyalty.

Judas also serves as treasurer for Team Jesus. And he is a dishonest one, often skimming funds from the community purse for his personal use. Though he sometimes pretends to care about the needs of the poor, his motives are selfish. This is because each time they give money to the poor, the balance in their fund drops, making it harder for Judas to steal from what is left.

Later, when Jesus eats the Passover meal with his disciples, he says that one of them will turn him in. When they wonder who, Jesus says it's the one he'll give the bread to. He dips the bread into something and hands it to Judas. Then Jesus tells Judas to "go do it quickly." The disciples miss this and assume Jesus is telling Judas to give money to the poor. Instead Judas leaves to lead the mob to arrest Jesus.

After Jesus is executed, grief overcomes Judas from the results of his actions. He hangs himself in remorse.

Had Judas not killed himself, might Jesus have offered mercy and restored him into right relationship with the group just like he did for Peter?

We serve a God who offers second chances, but do we forget that? Do we ever take God's second chances for granted?

[Discover more about Judas in Matthew 10:2–4, Matthew 27:1–10, John 12:4–6, and John 13:18–30.]

Nathanael

We've covered thirteen of Jesus's twelve disciples. Though not listed as one of the twelve, there is another follower of Jesus and a disciple. His name is Nathanael.

When Jesus invites Philip to "follow me," Philip goes and finds his good buddy, Nathanael.

"We found the one the prophets wrote about," Philip says. "His name is Jesus. He's from Nazareth."

"Nazareth!" Nathanael scoffs. "There's nothing good there."

"Come and check it out," Philip says. And they head off to find Jesus.

As they approach, Jesus says, "Now here's a true and honest Israelite."

"How can you possibly know me?" Nathanael asks.

"I saw you standing under the fig tree, before Philip came to tell you about me," Jesus says.

Nathanael's in awe. "Rabbi," he says, "surely you're the son of God, our king."

I imagine Jesus smiling as he replies. "You believe in me simply because I saw you under the fig tree? You'll see much more than that. Later, you'll see heaven open. Angels will descend and ascend from the Son of Man."

Nathanael follows Jesus and believes in him. Jesus promises that Nathanael will see amazing things. For this to happen, Nathanael will need to stick around. Though Nathanael may not be one of the twelve disciples, as Philip is, Nathanael is a follower of Jesus and witness to what he does.

How often do we wish we had a higher standing in church or ministry? Do we let that disappointment discourage us? Or do we push it aside and press on?

[Discover more about Nathanael in John 1:43–51.]

Centurion (1)

A centurion, a leader of one hundred soldiers in the Roman army, comes to Jesus for help. "My servant can't move," he says, "and is in great agony." The centurion doesn't ask Jesus to heal his servant.

Jesus asks him pointedly, "Do you want me to come and heal him?"

We expect the Centurion to answer just as directly and say, "Yes!" But he doesn't. Instead he says, "I'm not worthy for you to enter my house." Then he launches into an explanation about what he expects. "I'm a man under authority and who has authority. I tell my men what to do, and they do it." By implication the Centurion sees Jesus as having *spiritual* authority, able to just say the word and to heal the servant.

The Centurion's faith amazes Jesus, a faith greater than anyone he has met among his own people. Jesus then launches into a teaching about who's in and who's out in the kingdom of heaven. It's not what anyone anticipates, but Jesus seldom says or does what people expect.

After teaching about authority, faith, and salvation, Jesus turns to the centurion. "Go home. What you believed for has happened."

The servant is healed right then.

Later, after Jesus dies and rises from the dead, he gives his disciples all authority to overcome the power of the enemy—the same authority he used to heal the centurion's servant.

When Jesus gives his disciples all authority, how do we understand that? Do we have that authority today?

[Discover more about the centurion in Matthew 8:5–13 and Luke 7:1–10. Read about Jesus giving his disciples his authority in Luke 10:19.]

Four Friends of the Paralyzed Man

Matthew, Mark, and Luke all share a story about a paralyzed man whom Jesus heals. The man is the center of the story, but he plays a passive role. The only thing he does occurs *after* Jesus heals him, when he gets up and walks home.

The active participants in the story are the paralyzed man's four friends. Here's what happens.

When Jesus comes to town, the four friends believe that he can heal their paralyzed buddy. They act. They load him on a stretcher and carry him to the healer. But they can't reach Jesus. There are too many people, both inside the house and blocking the door. The simple response is to simply wait for Jesus to leave and ask for his help then. But they don't want to wait. They're desperate to help their friend walk. They lug him to the rooftop, make an opening, and lower him inside, right in front of Jesus. He sees *their* faith—not the faith of the paralyzed man.

What does Jesus do? He forgives the man for his mistakes. Though everyone thinks the man's greatest need is for his legs to work, Jesus knows better. He offers forgiveness instead.

The religious leaders are aghast. "Who is this arrogant man who thinks he can forgive sins?" they think.

Reading their minds, Jesus asks, "What's easier, to forgive someone or heal him?" To prove he can do both, he says, "Get up, pick up your mat, and go home."

The man does. The crowd buzzes in awe. They praise God.

The paralyzed man receives both forgiveness and healing through Jesus, not because of anything the man did, but because of his friends. They act. They bring him to Jesus, have faith, and persist in reaching him. What if they had encountered the crowds, given up, and gone home?

Do we take a passive role in life like the paralyzed man or take action like his four friends?

[Discover more about the paralyzed man and his friends in Matthew 9:2–8, Mark 2:1–12, and Luke 5:18–26.]

The Mother of James and John

Two of Jesus's disciples are James and John. Their father is Zebedee. He must have a booming voice because Mark calls James and John the Sons of Thunder. Pity their poor mom, married to a guy nicknamed Thunder. I imagine him as loud and overbearing, bold, without a hint of humility.

Yet James and John's mom must be a bit like her husband. She comes to Jesus and makes an audacious request for her boys. "Please let them sit in the places of honor in your kingdom, on your right and left."

Jesus is direct. "You don't realize what you're asking." He says only Papa can grant such a request. The other disciples are peeved at the brothers for their pushy mom.

However, we later see her bravely keeping vigil at the cross as Jesus dies. Matthew notes that she's one of the women who follows Jesus and cares for him. But we remember her most for being a pushy woman and her shameless effort to promote her boys.

Parents want the best for their kids. May God grant all parents the wisdom to know when to help them and when to let them grow up and fend for themselves.

Are we pushy or patient?

[Discover more about James and John's mom in Matthew 20:20–28 and Matthew 27:55–56. Read about the Sons of Thunder in Mark 3:17.]

Martha

M artha is the sister of Mary and Lazarus (1)—the man whom Jesus later raises from the dead. Though Jesus loves all people, the Bible specifically mentions that he loves Martha and her two siblings.

In reading what Luke and John write about Martha, we can make several assumptions: Martha owns her own home, likes to entertain, and has the gift of hospitality. She shows love by serving others. We can guess she may be older than her brother and sister.

The Bible shares two stories about Martha.

In one, she offers the most profound, faith-filled testimony about Jesus: "I believe you're the Messiah, the Son of God, who has come into the world." Her boldness and confidence inspire us. She declares this shortly before Jesus is executed. Unfortunately, this isn't what we best remember about her.

The other story happens earlier. She invites Jesus and his friends over for a meal. Amid her busy preparations, she complains to Jesus that her sister, Mary, isn't helping with the food. Instead, Mary is hanging out with Jesus.

In Jesus's surprising response, he affirms Mary for doing the best thing she can do and tells Martha to chill out. This perplexes me because if Martha followed her sister's example, no one would have anything to eat.

Another consideration, however, is Martha's misguided assumption that Mary should go along with her plans to feed Jesus and his squad. It's Martha's decision to invite Jesus over. Mary doesn't make that offer and has no obligation to help. Both sisters show their commitment to Jesus. They just do it in different ways.

How often do we expect others to automatically go along with our grand plans? Do we get mad when they don't jump in to help us?

[Discover more about Martha in Luke 10:38–42, John 11:5, 20–27, and John 12:2.]

Mary (3), Martha and Lazarus's Sister

Mary is the sister of Martha and Lazarus (1). The Bible includes two stories about her that cause me to label her as irresponsible. Jesus, however, has a different perspective.

In the first story, Mary sits at the feet of Jesus, listening to all he says. She basks in his presence while sister Martha toils in the kitchen. Martha complains about Mary's laziness, but Jesus puts Martha in her place. He affirms Mary for making the better choice.

In the second story, Mary takes some expensive perfume and pours it on Jesus's feet. Then she wipes them with her hair. This shows her love for him and symbolically prepares him for burial. Judas—who serves as the disciples' treasurer—criticizes her wasteful ways. He claims the perfume is worth one year's salary and should have been sold to help the poor. But Jesus rebuffs Judas. He says, "Mary did the right thing with her perfume, the thing she was meant to do. So don't hassle her."

Mary is first criticized for being lazy and later for being wasteful. But Jesus commends both actions.

Do we ever judge others from a human standpoint and miss God's perspective?

[Discover more about Mary in Luke 10:38–42 and John 12:2–3.]

Jairus

Jairus is a leader at the local synagogue. His twelve-year-old daughter is dying. He comes to Jesus and begs him to heal his little girl. Jesus agrees. However, he's delayed along the way when he stops to heal a woman with chronic bleeding.

Then word comes to Jairus that it's too late. His daughter is dead.

Jesus ignores their words and tells Jairus to just believe. Apparently Jairus does.

When Jesus arrives at Jairus's house, the mourning for his daughter's passing is already under way. Dismissing the crowd, he leads her parents and three disciples to her body. He takes the dead girl's hand and tells her to get up. Much to everyone's shock, she does. Then she walks around, very much alive.

We don't know what this girl experienced in the spiritual realm when she was dead or what her life in the physical realm was like afterwards. But she must certainly have lived with an appreciation for her father's strong faith and the knowledge that her second chance at life is because of Jesus's power over death.

The deep, unwavering faith of Jairus believes Jesus can heal his daughter. But Jesus does more. He provides the ultimate healing when he restores life into her lifeless body.

Do we have the kind of faith that raises the dead?

[Discover more about Jairus in Mark 5:22–42 and Luke 8:40–56.]

The Woman with Chronic Bleeding

For twelve years, a woman suffers from continuous bleeding. According to Jewish law, this makes her ceremonially unclean. Her condition limits how she functions in society and prohibits her from taking part in religious practices. For twelve years, this restricts her activities and interferes with her life.

She spends all her money on doctors, but none of them can help her. In fact, her bleeding gets worse.

In desperation, but with great faith, she believes Jesus can heal her.

She senses she need only touch his robe, that she doesn't need to even ask for his healing help. She worms her way through the throng and stretches out her hand to brush the hem of his robe. When she does, healing power leaves Jesus, and her bleeding stops. Her body is restored.

Though she thinks she does this in secret, Jesus knows. He stops. He demands to know who touched him. Unable to escape, she comes forward in trembling fear to confess what she did. Jesus affirms her faith, pronounces her healed, and sends her away in peace.

Do we believe in the healing power of Jesus?

[Discover more about this woman in Mark 5:25–34 and Luke 8:43–48. Read what the Jewish law says about bleeding in Leviticus 15:25–30.]

Zacchaeus

Zacchaeus is a tax collector in Jericho. But he's not just a tax collector. Luke says Zacchaeus is a *chief* tax collector. This likely means he's the manager of tax collectors or their leader, possibly skimming off the taxes they take in. Lest there be any doubt, Luke adds that he's wealthy. Oh, there's one more detail about Zacchaeus. He's short.

Zacchaeus wants to see Jesus, but he can't push his way through the crowd or see over all the taller people in front of him. Desperate to get a glimpse of Jesus, he has an idea. He runs down the road and scampers up a tree, a sycamore-fig tree.

Jesus approaches, and when he gets to the tree, he looks up. "Quick! Come down, Zacchaeus. I'm going to hang out with you at your house—today."

Zacchaeus climbs down and meets Jesus, welcoming him with gladness.

Though Zacchaeus is happy, the people aren't. Maybe they're jealous. They complain about Jesus planning to visit the home of a notorious man, a "sinner."

To prove that he's a changed man, Zacchaeus makes a bold pledge. "I'm going to give away half of everything I own to help poor people. And if I cheated anyone on their taxes, I'll reimburse them fourfold."

Jesus responds with the most astonishing promise, that Zacchaeus and his whole family are now saved.

What are we willing to do to show Jesus how much we love him? Though this may involve money, it could involve our time, priorities, or future.

[Discover more about Zacchaeus in Luke 19:1–10.]

The Rich Young Ruler

A young man, a rich ruler, rushes up to Jesus. The man asks what he must do to get into heaven. He's looking for the one step he's missing.

"Keep the commandments," Jesus says.

"Which ones?"

Jesus starts reeling off the Ten Commandments.

"Yep, I've kept every one of them since I was little," the man insists.

Then Jesus gets to the heart of the man's issues. "Only one thing remains," Jesus says. "Liquidate your assets and give away *everything*. Only then will heaven be what you value most. Then follow me."

The man's devastated. He expected Jesus would affirm him for his diligent obedience to the Law of Moses and the Ten Commandments.

That's not how Jesus sees it. Jesus sees a man who values his wealth, but his money is getting in the way of eternity. Jesus doesn't want people who rely on their money to follow him. He wants people who will rely on him more than anything else.

What this man seeks is confirmation that he's doing everything required. Instead Jesus offers correction.

What corrections is Jesus giving us? Which of our priorities is wrong and getting in our way of following Jesus?

[Discover more about this young man in Matthew 19:16–22, Mark 10:17–31, and Luke 18:18–30.]

James (3), the Brother of Jesus

We know Jesus has several brothers and sisters—half-brothers and sisters, sharing Mary as their mother. Remember, Jesus is the son of Mary and the Holy Spirit—God is his father—while his siblings are the offspring of Mary and Joseph.

One of Jesus's half-brothers is James. We don't read much about James during Jesus's lifetime, but a couple of accounts incriminate James.

First, John writes that even Jesus's own brothers don't believe him. That would include James.

Another time, the crowd keeps Jesus so busy that he can't even eat. His family hears about it and comes to get him. They think he's out of his mind, and they seek an intervention. Though Jesus's family, including James, is well-intended, they're also misguided. They see things from a human perspective, while Jesus holds a spiritual understanding.

So, James, as part of Jesus's family, doesn't believe him and tries to pull him away from his mission.

However, we later see Paul affirming Jesus's brother James as an apostle. And in Acts we see James leading the discussion about Gentile believers and determining how the church should move forward. That's quite a transformation.

James starts out doubting his brother Jesus and ends up leading his followers.

Do we accept that others can change, or do we view them according to their past?

[Discover more about James in Matthew 13:55, Mark 3:21, Mark 6:3, John 7:2–5, Acts 15:12–21, and Galatians 1:19.]

Herodias

Herod (2) is a powerful man. He gets what he wants. When he wants his brother's wife, Herodias, he takes her and marries her. John the Baptist publicly criticizes Herod for his actions. "What you did is wrong. You broke the Law of Moses."

For his boldness, John ends up in jail. Herod holds him there, keeping him out of public view, while at the same time protecting him from further harm.

We don't know if Herodias is the victim in this adulterous marriage or the instigator, but the Bible says she holds a grudge against John for his criticism. In fact, she's so enraged she wants him dead, but Herod won't allow it. He knows John is a good guy, and Herod likes to listen to him—even though John's words perplex him.

When Herod throws a birthday party for himself, Herodias's daughter dances for them. We don't know if her performance is offered or commanded. And we don't know what kind of dance this is. Is it an innocent expression of joy or a suggestive display of sexuality?

What we do know is that everyone likes her performance. Enamored—and without thinking—her stepdad promises to give her whatever she wants. She seeks Mom's advice. Herodias sees opportunity and responds fast. "Ask for John's head on a platter." The girl does.

Although sorely dismayed, Herod doesn't want to renege on his promise in front of his guests. To avoid public embarrassment, he orders John's immediate execution. They present John's head on a platter to the girl.

Blinded by anger, Herodias achieves her goal of orchestrating John's death. She uses her daughter to kill her enemy. She gets her revenge.

While we would never plot another person's death, Jesus says even anger toward another is akin to murder.

Do we commit that kind of murder? Have we ever used someone to accomplish our selfish goals?

[Discover more about Herodias in Matthew 14:3–12, Mark 6:17–28, and Luke 3:19–20.]

The Foreign Woman Who Doesn't Give Up

Jesus hangs out in Tyre, trying to rest, but folks track him down. One of the people who comes for help is a foreigner. While Matthew states she is from Canaan, Mark says she is a Greek, born in Syrian Phoenicia. Some people call her a Syrophoenician. Regardless of where she is from, the key point is that she isn't Jewish.

She has a little girl with a big issue. The girl's possessed by an impure spirit. Mom begs Jesus to heal her daughter and drive out the demon.

Jesus dismisses the woman. He says what the people expect, insinuating he came only to help Jewish people, not foreigners. In doing so, he implies that she's a dog, trying to eat the children's food, but he's creating a teachable moment.

The woman doesn't accept his apparent rebuff. She isn't offended by his seeming ethnic judgment. Quick to counter, she notes that even the dogs eat the crumbs that fall from the master's table.

Jesus affirms her wise reply. He pronounces the little girl healed. When Mom gets home, her daughter is resting in bed. The demon has left her body.

Now the people should realize that Jesus is there for everyone, both Jews and Gentiles. But they don't.

When we're rebuffed, do we accept it and give up or try even harder to achieve our goal? When God doesn't seem to listen to our pleas for help, do we stop asking or persist?

[Discover more about the foreign woman's story in Matthew 15:21–28 and Mark 7:24–30.]

The Poor Widow and Her Gift

J esus and his disciples stand near the temple as people come to give their money. They're people watching. One poor woman drops two small copper coins into the temple treasury. Her offering is so small. Surely it will do no good, unlike the considerable gifts of all the others.

Jesus sees things differently.

He pronounces her gift, though numerically small, as greater than everyone else's. "She put in more than all of them." Then Jesus explains. "They gave out of their abundance. She gave out of her poverty." He pauses and looks at his followers. "It was all she had to live on."

Imagine the penniless widow as she shuffles home. She just gave the last of her money to church. What will she eat? How will she live? Perhaps giving her last few cents was an impulse that she now regrets. Or maybe it was an intentional sacrifice that's still giving her joy. Regardless, what will tomorrow bring?

We don't know if God provides for her after she gives everything to him, but what we do know is that God doesn't consider the size of the gift as much as the heart of the giver.

How does God look upon our gifts? Do we give from our abundance or our poverty?

[Discover more about the poor widow in Mark 12:41–44 and Luke 21:1–4.]

The Samaritan Woman Fetching Water

The Jews dismiss Samaritans as half-breed misfits. Jews refuse to even associate with them. Even talking to one is social suicide. Yet Jesus defies convention, intentionally travels to one of their towns, and even stops there to rest. While he waits at the local well, he sends his disciples into town for food.

At noon, a Samaritan woman comes to draw water. She may pick this time to avoid seeing the other women of the village. Her life choices make her a social pariah. She's an outcast among outcasts.

Jesus surprises her by asking for a drink.

She's shocked.

Not only is he breaking conventions by talking with a hated Samaritan, and a woman no less, but he asks for a favor. If she gives him water, he will need to drink from her cup, another thing completely unacceptable to Jews.

Jesus, however, doesn't care what others think. He cares for her.

He also knows about her past, that she's been married five times and isn't married to the guy she's living with. Amazed that he knows her secrets, she affirms him as a prophet and later learns he is the Messiah everyone has been waiting for.

She goes and tells the villagers what Jesus said. Based on her testimony, they come out to meet him and believe. They ask him to hang out with them, and he stays for two days.

When we tell others about Jesus, is our story compelling enough for them to seriously consider him?

[Discover more about the Samaritan woman in John 4:5–42.]

Bartimaeus

Jesus heals many people who can't see, but we usually don't know their names. Bartimaeus is one exception. He lives in Jericho and is the son of Timaeus. That's all we know about him, except for the story of Jesus healing him.

Bartimaeus sits by the road begging for money, so he can get something to eat, else he might starve. Jesus and his entourage approach. Someone tells Bartimaeus who it is. "Jesus," Bartimaeus yells. "Help me!"

The crowd tries to hush him. He's annoying them.

But he just yells louder. "Jesus!"

Jesus stops and tells the crowd to fetch this blind beggar.

"It's your lucky day," they tell Bartimaeus. "Jesus is asking for you." Bartimaeus jumps up and comes to Jesus.

"What do you want?"

Bartimaeus states the obvious. "I want to see."

"Okay," Jesus says. "By your faith you are healed."

Then Bartimaeus can see. He follows Jesus down the road.

We don't hear of Bartimaeus again, so we don't know if he continues following Jesus for real. But we can revere God for the miracle Jesus performs for this once blind man.

Do we follow Jesus now like we once did? Do we still revere him?

[Discover more about Bartimaeus in Mark 10:46–52.]

Nicodemus

Nicodemus, a Pharisee and member of the Jewish Council, appears in three passages in the Bible. John writes all three. Clearly John wants us to know about Nicodemus. This is the only book that Nicodemus shows up in.

We first hear about Nicodemus when he comes to Jesus at night. This suggests he doesn't want his Pharisee friends and fellow Council members to know he's talking to a man that most religious leaders despise. They view Jesus as a heretic, an irritant, and a threat to their religion.

Though Nicodemus desperately wants to talk to Jesus, he's afraid of the repercussions if the religious hierarchy finds out. That's why he sneaks through the dark to find Jesus.

After Nicodemus commends Jesus for who he is and what he does, Jesus answers a question Nicodemus hasn't asked. Jesus says, "You must be born again if you hope to see the kingdom of God."

"What! How can a person be born a second time? Impossible."

Jesus launches into an intriguing explanation about being born of water *and* the spirit, about flesh birthing flesh and spirit birthing spirit. He talks about earthly things and heavenly things, about Moses lifting the bronze snake in the wilderness to save the people, and the Son of Man (Jesus) being lifted as well. "Everyone who believes in me will have eternal life."

Jesus ends by talking about truth and light, implying that Nicodemus needs to stop sneaking around in the dark. John doesn't record Nicodemus's response.

Later Jesus is arrested and brought before the Council. Nicodemus suggests that Jesus deserves a fair trial. Instead of following Nicodemus's wise advice, they verbally attack him.

A few days later, we see Nicodemus going with Joseph (from Arimathea) to give Jesus's body a proper burial.

These actions present risk for Nicodemus, physically and vocationally. Surely this suggests that Nicodemus supports Jesus and embraces his teaching.

What risks are we willing to take for Jesus?

[Discover more about Nicodemus in John 3:1–21, John 7:45–52, and John 19:38–42. Learn about the bronze snake in Numbers 21:9.]

Luke

L uke, the only non-Jewish author in the New Testament, writes as an outsider looking in. This gives his writing a perspective that most non-Jewish Christians embrace, because we, too, are outsiders. Luke writes the two longest books in the New Testament. They make up about 25 percent of the New Testament's content. Only Paul is more prolific.

The first book Luke writes is his biography of Jesus, called The Gospel of Luke or simply Luke. Luke researches his subject and interviews eyewitnesses. He records his findings for Theophilus.

In Luke's second piece, he continues his investigation, chronicling the early church. We call this book The Acts of the Apostles, the book of Acts, or simply Acts.

Again Luke documents his findings for Theophilus. At some points in the narrative, Luke participates in the events he covers. We see this when he switches from third person to first person, using the pronouns *I* and *we*.

Many people appreciate Luke's writing style for the details he mentions that aren't in the other three biographies of Jesus. Aside from this, we know little about

Luke. His name only appears three times in the Bible, each time toward the end of one of Paul's letters.

In Paul's letter to the church in Colossae, he calls Doctor Luke a dear friend who sends greetings to the Colossians. It's likely that Luke is with Paul when he writes that letter.

Next, in Paul's personal letter to his protégé Timothy, Paul dips into a bit of despair, writing that "Only Luke is still with me."

Then, in Paul's letter to Philemon, he calls Luke a fellow worker for the cause of Jesus.

From these we see Luke as a dear friend, loyal companion, and faithful missionary.

Luke does much to help us better understand Jesus, but he receives little credit. Are we willing to do the same?

[Discover more about Luke in Colossians 4:14, 2 Timothy 4:11, and Philemon 1:24.]

Theophilus

As mentioned in the previous chapter on Luke, we know he writes twice to Theophilus and that these letters are part of the Bible in the books of Luke and Acts.

Though the Bible tells us nothing about Theophilus, Luke addresses both his letters to this mysterious person. The reason is significant. Luke wants Theophilus to know for certain the things he had been taught about Jesus.

Think about this.

Someone tells Theophilus about Jesus. Perhaps Theophilus believes, but maybe he isn't fully convinced. He might carry a tinge of doubt about this Jesus, the man who changed religion into a relationship. It's so countercultural that it's revolutionary. Regardless, Luke feels it's worth his time to help Theophilus know Jesus for sure.

This is a huge undertaking for Luke. He spends a great deal of time researching the subject and more time writing his findings—all for Theophilus.

Luke's biography of Jesus is the longest book in the New Testament, at just under 20,000 words. His sequel, the book of Acts, is the second longest. Together they're almost the length of a short novel. That's a lot of words, a lot of writing, and a lot of research.

Though Luke writes this book for one person, Theophilus, it's available for us two thousand years later. Like Theophilus, we too can read Luke's account of Jesus so that we can know for certain the things we've been taught.

How much effort will we make to help one person know Jesus for sure?

[Discover more about Theophilus in Luke 1:1–4 and Acts 1:1–2.]

Joanna

J oanna only appears in Luke's biography of Jesus. And then just twice, but we can learn much from what Luke writes about her.

First, she, along with several other women, helps care for Jesus and support his work. More on this later.

Next, Joanna also joins Mary Magdalene and Mary the mother of James and John (remember, they're the Sons of Thunder) in wanting to embalm Jesus's body, which they don't get to do since he rises from the dead.

A third thing we know about Joanna is that Jesus casts demons out of her, along with Mary Magdalene, Susanna, and several others. Jesus relieves them of their afflictions. Joanna's response is to do what she can for him.

Now, on to the good part.

The fourth thing about Joanna, which is both significant and easy to overlook, is that she's married to Chuza. Why does this matter?

Chuza manages the household of Herod (2). Again, huh?

Here's why: Herod opposes Jesus. Chuza works for Herod. Herod pays Chuza. Chuza's wife, Joanna, gives money to support Jesus. This means that in an indirect way Herod financially supports Jesus. If Herod knew, he'd surely explode in anger.

When God blesses us with money or possessions, what we do with them matters.

Are we using the money God blesses us with to help others?

[Discover more about Joanna in Luke 8:1–3 and Luke 24:1–11.]

The Women Who Anoint Jesus

Each of the four biographies of Jesus—Matthew, Mark, Luke, and John— include a story about a woman who anoints Jesus with expensive perfume, but the details in each report vary. It may be that this happens on four separate occasions. Or it could be the same story, with a few details that differ. Or it may be somewhere in between, with there being two or three times that women anoint Jesus.

Looking at all four accounts, what they share is that a woman comes up to Jesus and pours some expensive perfume on him. Her extravagant act generates criticism. These are the main points of the story.

The details that differ are where this takes place, the identity of the woman, and where she anoints him (on his head or his feet). Two other misaligned items are who is present when this occurs and who criticizes her for this wasteful action.

These details aren't as relevant as the theme of the story. The key point is that this woman (or women) gives us an example of lavish adoration of Jesus. She worships him in the most extravagant way she can.

How extravagant *is our worship of Jesus? Are we free to worship him regardless of what others say or think?*

[Discover more about the women who anoint Jesus in Matthew 26:6–13, Mark 14:3–9, Luke 7:36–50, and John 12:1–8.]

Simon (5) the Pharisee

In Luke's account of the woman who pours her perfume on Jesus, Luke says it happens at the house of Simon, a Pharisee. Luke also records the interesting exchange between Simon and Jesus that isn't in the other three biographies of Jesus.

In this account, Luke writes that it's Simon who levies the criticism, but it's not directed at the woman who pours her perfume on Jesus, it's against Jesus. Simon doesn't denounce Jesus out loud. He merely thinks it. He feels Jesus should have known the woman is a sinner and stopped her from touching him.

Perceiving Simon's thoughts, Jesus turns to him. "Suppose two people owe money to a moneylender. One owes a couple hundred bucks and the other only twenty. Neither one can pay him back, so the lender writes off both loans. Which of the two people will be more appreciative?"

"The one with the larger debt," Simon says.

"You're right." Then Jesus turns to the woman. "See her," Jesus says. "When I came into your home you didn't wash my feet as is the custom, greet me with a kiss, or anoint my head with oil, but this woman has washed my feet with her tears, not stopped kissing my feet, and anointed them with perfume. Though she has done many wrong things in her life, she's most grateful for having been forgiven."

As the people murmur about Jesus forgiving her sins, he has one more thing to say to her, "By your faith, you're saved. Now go in peace."

How grateful are we to Jesus? Should we be more grateful than we are?

[Discover more about Simon the Pharisee in Luke 7:36–47.]

Lazarus (1)

azarus is the brother of Martha and Mary (3). The Bible writers give more attention to Mary and Martha, but we can only speculate why. It may be that Lazarus is the younger brother, possibly not even an adult. Maybe he just doesn't do anything worth mentioning, but the one story about him in the Bible is a story that most people know.

It starts with Lazarus getting sick. This isn't a cold, flu, or eating too much of the wrong thing. This is a serious "go get Jesus because Lazarus might die" situation.

Martha and Mary send word to Jesus: "The one you love is sick."

Even though the Bible says that Jesus loves the three siblings, he doesn't drop everything to pay them a visit and heal the ailing Lazarus. He waits two days. Then he heads out.

By the time Jesus arrives, it's too late—or is it? Lazarus has been dead four days and is already entombed.

Martha reaches Jesus first and criticizes him. "If only you'd been here, he wouldn't have died." Yet she clings to a glimmer of hope. "Even so, God will do whatever you ask."

Jesus promises her that Lazarus will rise again. Though Jesus means now, Martha thinks he means at the end of time. Then Jesus says, "I am resurrection, and I am life. Do you believe?"

Martha affirms Jesus as the Messiah, the Son of God.

Then Mary shows up and criticizes Jesus, just like her sister.

"Where's he buried?" Jesus asks.

As the sisters take Jesus to the tomb, he cries.

"Open the burial vault," Jesus commands.

After some debate about how bad the decaying body will smell, they do as Jesus requests.

Jesus gives a prayer of thanksgiving to Papa. Then he calls, "Lazarus. Come out!"

Lazarus does, still wrapped with burial cloths.

Thanks to Jesus, Lazarus has a second chance at life.

Through Jesus, we all have second chances. What are we doing with ours?

[Discover more about Lazarus in John 11:1–44 and John 12:1.]

Part 3:

———∿∿———

The Victory of Jesus

For the next section of *The Friends and Foes of Jesus*, we'll look at the short time from his arrest to his resurrection. Consider Jesus's interactions with each person he encounters.

How do they react to him? How does their life change?

Malchus

Each of the biographies of Jesus include the story of a mob coming up to Jesus to arrest him. In each account one of Jesus's disciples whips out a sword and slashes at the high priest's servant, cutting off his ear.

Why is the high priest's servant there? He could be acting on his own accord, though more likely the high priest ordered him to join the mob tasked with arresting Jesus. The bigger the crowd, the easier this will be. This implicates the high priest in the conspiracy to arrest and execute Jesus.

By combining these four biblical accounts of this event, we discover that the high priest's servant's name is Malchus. We also learn that the assaulting disciple is Peter. Given what we know about him this shouldn't surprise us. He often speaks before thinking and sometimes acts just as fast.

What's most delightful, however, is a detail that only Luke shares. After Jesus tells his disciples to not resist his arrest, he restores Malchus's missing ear. Even when Jesus faces arrest, setting in motion the events that will lead to his death, he still cares about the needs of others.

When we face difficulties, do we still notice the not-as-important needs of those around us?

[Discover more about Malchus in Matthew 26:47–52, Mark 14:43–50, Luke 22:49–51, and John 18:10–11.]

Barabbas

Barabbas appears in one scene in each of the Bible's four biographies of Jesus. We know little about Barabbas except that he's in prison for insurrection and murder. He's certainly not one of the good guys. Because he's held on murder charges, he may face crucifixion. He's probably on death row awaiting his execution, perhaps even as soon as Passover ends.

Then Jesus comes along.

Isn't this the pivotal moment in a lot of people's lives?

Jesus has been arrested, and the Jewish leaders want to do away with him. But Pilate tries to bring about Jesus's release. Pilate's findings don't matter to the mob, and his attempts to broker a less deadly solution get nowhere. Whipped into a frenzy, the people don't care about the law or about justice. They want blood.

Pilate's custom each Passover is to release a prisoner, as requested by the people. This gives him an opportunity to earn some goodwill from the Jews who hate him and the Roman rule he represents.

Knowing that the Jewish leaders are railroading Jesus, Pilate offers to release him this year. The mob will have none of it. Instead they shout their request, "Barabbas!"

They don't want Jesus—who came to heal and save—freed. Instead they want a murderer released back into society. This makes no sense, but mobs never do.

Unable to dissuade them and wanting to avoid a riot, Pilate releases Barabbas and hands Jesus over for crucifixion. Barabbas, who deserves death, is set free, and Jesus, who is without fault, dies instead. We don't hear anything more about Barabbas after this, so we're left to wonder how he reacts to the second chance Jesus gives him by dying in his place.

Are we truly thankful that Jesus died for us? What do we do to let him know?

[Discover more about Barabbas in Matthew 27:15–26, Mark 15:6–15, Luke 23:18–19, and John 18:39–40.]

Caiaphas

We recognize Caiaphas as a central player in the unethical, corrupt, and self-seeking plot that results in the crucifixion of Jesus. Caiaphas's name shows up in the writings of Matthew, Luke, and John. Though we don't know much about him, here's what we are aware of.

First, he's the high priest—the main man—when the religious leaders railroad Jesus into a wrongful execution.

Next, he's the son-in-law of another high priest, Annas.

Third, he's most likely rich. Matthew writes that the religious leaders meet at Caiaphas's palace to develop a scheme to do away with Jesus. We can suspect that Caiaphas, like other highly-placed, influential religious leaders, is well-off. However, knowing he lives in a palace suggests just how financially lucrative the high priesthood is.

Caiaphas and the other religious leaders see Jesus as a threat to the prestige, power, and possessions they've amassed through their religious positions. They want to stop Jesus—not so much because of his theology—but because they fear losing their wealth, influence, and public respect.

Jesus must die.

Given all this, it's easy to see Caiaphas as a villain. And though he is, another passage lets us see him as a prophet, one supernaturally influenced.

After Jesus raises Lazarus (1) from the dead, the religious leaders hold an emergency meeting of the governing board, the Sanhedrin. Frustrated with Jesus, they wonder what to do. Then Caiaphas speaks up. "You don't get it!" he says. "Let's have one man die for all the people, instead of putting the whole country at risk."

Caiaphas doesn't say this on his own, John notes, but he prophesies of Jesus's sacrificial death to save his people.

Are we willing to see good things in otherwise bad people?

[Discover more about Caiaphas in Matthew 26:3–5, Matthew 26:57, Luke 3:1–2, John 11:49–52, John 18:12–14, John 18:24, and Acts 4:5–6.]

Annas

Annas is a priest, the father-in-law of another priest, Caiaphas. At various points they both serve as the high priest. As we read the narrative in the Bible, sometimes Annas is the high priest and other times Caiaphas is.

Luke implies that the pair form an era of high-priesthood rule. Together they work as a leadership team that wields power when John the Baptist starts his ministry, exists when Jesus is executed, and is still around during the early church.

In John's biography of Jesus, he writes that after Jesus's arrest, the mob drags him to stand before Annas, who is the high priest. After the officials abuse and mock Jesus, Annas sends Jesus to his son-in-law, Caiaphas. John also identifies Caiaphas as the high priest at this point. This suggests they might have a co-reign in leading the Jewish religious institution and influencing the culture.

The final time we read of Annas is when Peter and John stand before the religious Council (the Sanhedrin). Again, Annas is the high priest. Caiaphas is there too, along with a couple other members of their family. Annas oversees the proceedings. After Peter and John make their defense, which is really them sharing the good news about Jesus to the religious leaders, the Council doesn't know what to do.

Under Annas's leadership they command Peter and John to stop telling others about Jesus and issue threats if they do. However, the Council decides not to punish them because of the people's astonishment over Peter's healing of the disabled man.

Annas, along with his son-in-law, Caiaphas, wields control over the Jewish people and their faith. As leaders they could have embraced Jesus and his message. Instead they oppose it and try to squelch it. They abuse their power.

When we're in charge of something, what do we do to make sure our decisions and actions align with God's will?

[Discover more about Annas in Luke 3:1–2, John 18:12–14, John 18:24, and Acts 4:5–6.]

Herod (2)

Two guys named Herod appear in Jesus's story. The first Herod (1) attempts to kill Jesus shortly after he's born. The second Herod (2) plays a part in Jesus's death.

But before we discuss that, let's look at some other things Herod (2) does. Remember Herodias? She's married to Herod, after he takes her from her first husband, his brother. Strike one for Herod taking his sibling's spouse.

John the Baptist criticizes their marriage, and Herod tosses him in prison. Strike two for Herod punishing an innocent man.

Then Herodias uses a situation with her daughter to manipulate Herod into killing John. Though Herod could and should have said "no," he gives in and orders the beheading of John. Strike three for killing a guiltless man.

The next time we hear of Herod is when Jesus is being railroaded into his execution. Luke writes that Herod had wanted to see Jesus and is pleased Pilate sends Jesus to him. Herod hopes to witness a miracle and asks Jesus many questions, but he doesn't answer. Then Herod mocks Jesus before sending him back to Pilate.

Herod didn't need to do that. He could have kept Jesus under his jurisdiction and saved him from death. Instead Herod takes the easy way out and sends Jesus back to Pilate.

Have we ever avoided doing what was right and taken the easy way out?

[Discover more about Herod in Matthew 14:1–12 and Mark 6:14–28.]

Pilate

While we look at Caiaphas as instrumental in bringing about the decision that Jesus must die, it's Pilate—occasionally called Pontius Pilate—who has the authority to make it happen. Though Caiaphas gets things rolling, Pilate—although he tries to stop Jesus's execution—allows the proceedings to gather momentum.

After arresting Jesus and deciding he must die, the religious Council drags him to Pilate. They levy their ill-founded accusations against Jesus, but they can't convince Pilate.

"I find him innocent," Pilate says.

The Jewish leaders persist.

Then Pilate, learning that Jesus is from Galilee, sees a way out. He sends Jesus to Herod (2) who has jurisdiction over Galilee. Herod happens to be in Jerusalem, likely for the Passover. Wanting to meet Jesus, Herod asks him many questions—which he doesn't answer—but then mocks him before sending him back to Pilate.

A second time Pilate tries to release Jesus.

A mob forms. They don't want Jesus set free. They ask Pilate to release Barabbas instead. They shout for Jesus's execution.

Unable to quiet the throng and unwilling to risk making them angrier by releasing Jesus, Pilate gives in to their demands. But first he washes his hands in front of them to symbolically claim he's innocent of Jesus's death.

Pilate has a sign placed on the cross, which says "The king of the Jews." Though the Jewish leaders object to his wording, Pilate won't budge. Perhaps this is his small way to have the final word. But how much better would it have been for him to have done the right thing and protected Jesus from an unjust death?

When faced with a tough situation, do we do what's right or give in to the pressure of others?

[Discover more about Pilate in Matthew 27, Mark 15, and John 18:28–19:38.]

Simon (6) from Cyrene

Another biblical character who only appears in one scene in the Bible (albeit in three different books) is a man we know as Simon. He comes from Cyrene—as in Simon from Cyrene. Simon is a man who is in the wrong place at the wrong time.

According to the practice of crucifixion, the soldiers make Jesus carry his own cross to the site of his execution. In his weakened state, from the beatings and abuse heaped upon him, he's not able to do so. The soldiers certainly don't want to lug this heavy instrument of death through the city streets, so they grab someone and force him to do it. The man's name is Simon.

Other than knowing where Simon comes from and him being a victim of bad timing, we know one more thing about him. He has two boys: Alexander and Rufus. Aside from these things, we know nothing else about him. We can only wonder.

Is he a friend of Jesus or a foe? Does he see his forced labor as a service to his Savior or helping to end the life of a man who the Jewish leaders deride as a heretic?

We also don't know what happens to Simon afterwards. Is his life forever changed because of his brief meeting with Jesus? Does he feel guilt for his unwilling role in bringing about the death of an innocent man?

Perhaps Simon ends up following Jesus. We can hope so, that his encounter with Jesus changes his life forever.

When we encounter Jesus, what is our response?

[Discover more about Simon from Cyrene in Matthew 27:32, Mark 15:21, and Luke 23:26.]

Two Criminals on the Cross

Two criminals are executed with Jesus. Luke records a significant detail that doesn't appear in the other biographies of Jesus. As the three of them hang on their crosses, they have a conversation. If I were enduring the pain of torturous death, I doubt I'd say anything, but these three men talk to each other.

The first criminal says, "You're the savior, right? Why don't you save yourself—and us too?"

But the second criminal has a different perspective. He criticizes the first guy. "What's wrong with you? We're getting what we deserve, but Jesus is innocent." Then he says to Jesus, "Please remember me when you begin ruling in your kingdom."

Jesus responds with the most amazing, confusing, and comforting answer. "Today you will hang out with me in heaven."

This second criminal merely affirms Jesus's innocence and asks to be with him. He doesn't repent or do any of the things most religious people insist we must do to go to heaven. Even so, Jesus offers him mercy and promises him a place in paradise. How cool is that?

Compare the second criminal to the first. The first one recognizes Jesus as the savior, the messiah that the people have been waiting for. He even asks Jesus to save him. However, Jesus doesn't physically save him, and I doubt he spiritually saves him either.

We could interpret Jesus's promise of "you will be with me" as a plural you and apply it to both criminals, as in "you all will be with me," but I think Jesus directs his salvation comment only to the second criminal, who admits his mistakes and the appropriateness of his punishment.

Both criminals recognize Jesus for his saving power, and both ask him for help, but only one admits his faults. Is that what makes the difference?

If the second criminal's conversion doesn't fit our idea of salvation, what do we need to change in our understanding?

[Discover more about the two criminals in Luke 23:39–43.]

Joseph (6) from Arimathea

After Jesus dies, Joseph from Arimathea provides for the burial of Jesus. We don't know much about this Joseph, but we do know three facts.

First, he's wealthy, rich enough to have his own rock-hewn burial vault on his property.

Next, he is a member—a prominent one—of the Jewish Council, waiting in expectation for the coming of God's kingdom.

Third, and most importantly, Joseph is a disciple of Jesus—albeit secretly, out of fear for what would happen to him if other Council members find out.

Not wanting to see Jesus's body suffer the indignity of hanging on the cross over the Sabbath, Joseph seeks permission from Pilate to take down the body and give Jesus a proper burial.

This tells us one more thing about Joseph. He is bold when it matters.

Though he may have been cautious with what he revealed about his personal beliefs to the Council in the past, requesting Jesus's body for burial clearly shows Joseph's alliance with Jesus. There is now no doubt about Joseph's loyalty.

In making his position public, Joseph risks much. He could be kicked off the Council, ostracized from society, and suffer death, just like Jesus. Though we don't know if any of these things take place, we also don't read anything more about Joseph in the Bible.

How much of our position, power, and prestige are we willing to risk if we let everyone know we've gone all in for Jesus?

[Discover more about Joseph from Arimathea in Matthew 27:57–60, Mark 15:42–46, and John 19:38–42.]

Mary (2) Magdalene

Recent public opinion about Mary Magdalene hasn't been kind, with people making unfounded assumptions about her. Some think she's a prostitute or accuse her of an immoral lifestyle, but we don't find that in the Bible—unless we try connecting dots that don't align.

What the Bible does say is that Jesus casts seven demons out of her. Regardless of how we understand this, we know that he makes her life much better.

In response, Mary Magdalene shows her gratitude by following Jesus. She also helps support him financially. Later she's there, along with a few other women, when Jesus dies and then when he's buried. The next day, she leads a group to his tomb to properly prepare his body, according to the customs of the day. Of course, they can't do this because Jesus's body isn't there. Angels tell her Jesus has risen from the dead, that he's alive.

Later Jesus appears to her and tells her to let the disciples know.

This is significant because a woman's testimony isn't legally accepted in that culture. However, to underscore God's affirmation of women, Jesus has Mary Magdalene deliver the breaking news of the most significant event in human history. This marks her—a female—as the first apostle added after Jesus's death.

Like Mary Magdalene, people sometimes think or say things about us that aren't true. While this can hurt deeply, it's God's opinion that counts.

If our conscience is clear with God, what people say shouldn't matter. But does it anyway?

[Discover more about Mary Magdalene in Matthew 27:55–28:10, Luke 8:1–2, Luke 24:1–10, John 19:25, and John 20:1–18.]

Part 4:

The Early Church in Acts

I n the next section of *The Friends and Foes of Jesus*, we'll look at his disciples and their opponents as they move forward to organize his followers and launch the church that his ministry started. In these we see a mixture of faith and fear, along with some misunderstanding and disagreement. But through them all we get a glimpse into who we are, who we should be, and who we can become through Jesus. First, we'll cover people that pop up in the Acts narrative.

Matthias

After Jesus's death, his betrayer, Judas, is filled with remorse and commits suicide. The twelve disciples are now only eleven in number. Peter stands before them and quotes two passages from Psalms. The second verse says, "May someone else replace him." Though this may seem vague to us, the eleven disciples see this as a command—or a prophetic word—to find a replacement for Judas.

To do this they nominate two men who followed Jesus, from his baptism through to his ascension. They seek men who know all about Jesus and his ministry, including his resurrection from the dead. (Unfortunately, the verse specifies men. Personally, I would have loved for them to have considered Mary Magdalene as the twelfth disciple.)

They nominate two men: Barsabbas (1) and Matthias. To us, the next logical step is to vote. But they don't. Instead they pray for God—who knows everyone's hearts—to choose which man should take the place of Judas. Then, in faith, they cast lots, believing that the winner is God's choice. The lot falls to Matthias. Again, we have twelve disciples.

What's perplexing is that this is the last time we hear about Matthias. We don't know if he becomes a loyal disciple or fizzles out. We don't know if he helps advance the kingdom of God or abandons the cause. Does he finish strong or falter?

What do we need to do to make sure we finish strong for Jesus?

[Discover more about Matthias in Acts 1:15–26.]

Barsabbas (1)

As we covered in the last chapter, Matthias and Barsabbas are both nominated to become the twelfth disciple, a role only one of them can fill. They each have the needed credentials, having hung out with the disciples for three years, starting with Jesus's baptism through to his return to heaven. They also both witnessed Jesus's resurrection, his victory over death.

We don't know anything else about Barsabbas, except that he has a couple of other names too: Joseph (7) and Justus.

As mentioned, both men are qualified, but only one can be chosen.

Though voting seems the fair way—the democratic approach—the disciples have a better idea. Instead of letting people decide, they're going to let God pick. To do this they will draw straws (literally, they'll throw dice). They do this with prayerful confidence that God will cause the person he wants to draw the long straw.

Barsabbas gets a short straw. Bummer.

God picks Matthias over him.

How humiliating for Barsabbas. We're left to wonder how he reacts. Does he stomp off in a huff, mad that God selected someone else, or does he push forward in faith, striving to overcome this disappointment?

We do encounter the name Barsabbas again in the Bible—fully engaged and elevated to a leadership position—but we don't know if this is the same man or not. It's perplexing because this Barsabbas has a different nickname: Judas.

Personally, I want this to be the same man. It gives me hope that if we persevere in faith, we can overcome disappointment and be used by God later.

How can we respond to profound disappointment in a way that honors God?

[Discover more about Barsabbas in Acts 1:21–26 and Acts 15:22.]

Barnabas

We know Joseph (8) better as Barnabas. That's the name the apostles give him. It means "son of encouragement," which is a great nickname because he serves as a mentor and encourages others. The Bible records two occasions when he does this, and there are probably many others we aren't aware of.

Barnabas's first mentee is Saul (2). After Saul's conversion, the disciples in Jerusalem are understandably afraid of him, but Barnabas helps Saul get plugged in.

The disciples send Barnabas to Antioch as their first missionary. When he sees how the Holy Spirit is at work there, he finds Saul and the two of them work in Antioch for an entire year. Barnabas is Saul's mentor. Without Barnabas, Saul may have never been connected to the church and learned how to help it grow. Eventually, the dynamics of the relationship shift, with Saul (later known as Paul) taking a lead role in their partnership.

The pair continues to travel, tell others about Jesus, and establish churches. Then Barnabas wants to take his nephew, John Mark, with them, but Paul doesn't. This is because Mark deserted them on a prior trip. Barnabas and Paul argue about what to do, and their ministry breaks up over their disagreement.

Though their split is disappointing, it serves to double their effectiveness. Barnabas takes Mark, to mentor him, and they head for Cyprus. Saul picks Silas as his mentee, and they head for Syria.

Though Barnabas and Saul made a good team, it's time for them to mentor others.

How can we decide when we should leave something that's good to pursue something that might be even better?

[Discover more about Barnabas in Acts 4:36–37, Acts 9:26–28, Acts 11:22–26, Acts 13–15 (especially Acts 15:36–41), Galatians 2:1–14, and Colossians 4:10.]

Ananias (1) and Sapphira

Ananias and his wife, Sapphira, sell some land and give the proceeds to the church. A lot of Jesus's more well-to-do followers are doing the same thing.

However, Ananias and Sapphira keep some of the money for themselves. They're free to do this. But they claim their donation is the full amount of the sale. They're liars and posers.

Peter confronts Ananias about his duplicity. Ananias drops dead. There's no mercy offered, no second chance given, and no investigation conducted. In this case, God's judgment is swift and final. Some of the men in their community bury him.

A few hours later, not knowing the fate of her husband, Sapphira shows up. Peter confronts her as well. Again, there's no mercy, second chance, or investigation. She, too, falls dead. The men who just buried Ananias then bury her.

A holy fear grips the church.

We seldom suffer immediate punishment for the wrong things we do. This delay could cause us to assume judgment won't happen. But without Jesus's saving power, punishment is inevitable.

Ananias and Sapphira agree to deceive Peter and the church of Jesus. More significantly, they lie to the Holy Spirit. In their case, lying to the Holy Spirit is punishable by death—an immediate death.

We need to guard against doing wrong, especially about lying to the Holy Spirit.

[Discover more about Ananias and Sapphira in Acts 5:1–11.]

Gamaliel (2)

Gamaliel is a Pharisee and teacher of the Jewish law. He trained young Saul, who studied under him. All the people respect him for his wisdom and character. The Bible gives us one story about Gamaliel.

Some of the religious leaders grow jealous of the influence Peter and the other apostles have on the people. After the apostles' arrest and miraculous release from prison, they head back to the temple to teach about Jesus. They're rounded up again and brought before the religious Council. "We explicitly told you to stop talking about Jesus," the high priest says, "but you persist, even trying to pin his death on us."

"We must obey God and not you," Peter says. Then he launches into a mini sermon. His words infuriate the Council, who want to silence him and his crew permanently.

But wise Gamaliel intervenes. The Council goes into a private session and Gamaliel warns them that they should proceed with much caution. He reviews some historical examples of leaders who popped on the scene, built a following, and then died. Their followers scattered.

"My recommendation is to leave these men alone. If they're acting on their own, their movement will fail. But if they're acting on God's authority, we'll never stop them and will find ourselves fighting against God."

This persuades the Council to not take excessive action. They have the apostles beaten and let them go with a warning.

When we encounter things that challenge our theology, what should we do to make sure our opposition to these ideas doesn't cause us to end up fighting against God?

[Discover more about Gamaliel in Acts 5:33–42 and Acts 22:3.]

Stephen

As Jesus's church grows, it becomes hard for the twelve disciples to manage the practical needs of their followers and still do their main job. To focus on teaching, they decide to find seven godly men to help with the fair distribution of food. (Sorry ladies, again the Bible specifies men, but don't let this past cultural convention limit what you do today.) One of the seven is Stephen. He's a man of great faith and full of the Holy Spirit.

Stephen, under God's grace and power, performs many amazing miracles. But some people oppose him and argue with him. Unable to counter Stephen's wisdom, some men slander him. They accuse him of blasphemy. This riles up the crowd, and they drag him before the religious Council. For their prosecution, Stephen's detractors present more false witnesses.

As they prosecute Stephen, his face glows like an angel. He launches into a powerful sermon, reviewing his people's history up to the present time. He collectively calls them uncircumcised (a huge religious insult at that time) and says they resist the Holy Spirit. He says their ancestors murdered the prophets who predicted Jesus's coming. "And now you killed him."

Furious, they grind their teeth at him.

"Hey, look." Stephen points up. "I see heaven and Jesus standing there at God's right hand."

They cover their ears so they can't hear him, scream as loud as they can, and rush him. They drag him out of town and throw stones at him.

As Stephen's life fades, he gives his spirit over to Jesus and asks that the men killing him not be held guilty for their actions. Then he dies.

A young Pharisee named Saul sees the whole thing, and he approves of Stephen's murder.

When people do us harm, how far will we go to ask God to forgive them?

[Discover more about Stephen in Acts 6:1–8:2, Acts 11:19, and Acts 22:20.]

Philip (3)

Philip (1) is a disciple of Jesus, whereas Philip (3) is a deacon in the early church, chosen with seven others to manage their growing community. In addition to helping run the church in Jerusalem, Philip is also an evangelist.

When persecution hits the church in Jerusalem and the people scatter to avoid arrest or execution, Philip heads to Samaria to tell them about Jesus. He performs supernatural acts, which gets their attention. He casts out evil spirits and heals people in the city. There's a revival, and joy fills the people.

In the middle of this, God sends an angel to Philip. "Leave all this and head south into the desert." What? Great things are happening in Samaria, so it makes no sense to send Philip into the desert where there are no people to tell about Jesus. But Philip obeys.

There he sees an important official from Ethiopia, heading home in his chariot. The Holy Spirit tells Philip to approach the man, which he does. The man is reading the writings of the prophet Isaiah.

"Do you understand it?" Philip asks.

Though the man is trying to make sense of it, he can't. He invites Philip to join him in his chariot. Philip hops up. The passage is a prophecy about Jesus. Philip explains everything. When they come to some water, the man asks Philip to baptize him.

Philip does, and then God's spirit whisks Philip away and brings him to Azotus.

The next time we see Philip, it's in Caesarea. Paul and his team stay at Philip's home. In this passage we learn one more thing about Philip. He has four daughters who have the gift of prophecy. No doubt, Philip's godly influence on his girls help them grow in their faith and develop this gift.

What can we do to have a godly impact on our children and those within our influence?

[Discover more about Philip in Acts 6:2–5, Acts 8:4–40, and Acts 21:8–9.]

The Ethiopian Treasurer

A man from Ethiopia makes a pilgrimage to Jerusalem. He's a high-ranking official in the Ethiopian government, the treasurer to the Kandake, the Queen of the Ethiopian people. The Bible also tells us that he's a eunuch. This doesn't seem relevant, yet we pin this label on this man calling him the Ethiopian eunuch. But this makes me squirm, so I'll call him the Ethiopian treasurer instead.

Taking a leave of absence from work, he travels to Jerusalem to worship God. Then he heads home. It's a long journey, but he has his chariot to make the trip easier and faster. Along the way, he pulls out a scroll and reads from Isaiah's prophecy. Though intrigued, he can't quite make sense of it.

That's when this Jewish guy, Philip, strolls up and asks if he has any questions.

Boy, does he. The passage is a prophetic look at Jesus, but the man can't wrap his mind around it. "Is Isaiah talking about himself or someone else?"

Building on that passage, Philip tells the Ethiopian treasurer all about Jesus. Then things start to click. They travel along the road as Philip teaches. When they come to some water, the man asks Philip to baptize him. Philip agrees, but when the man rises out of the water, Philip is gone. Unshaken, the Ethiopian treasurer continues his journey home, full of much joy for what God has done for him through Jesus.

If some unexplainable, supernatural thing happens to us, do we dismiss it or praise God?

[Discover more about the Ethiopian treasurer in Acts 8:26–39.]

Simon (8) the Sorcerer

In the city of Samaria, lives Simon. He's a sorcerer, a wizard of sorts who amazes people with his supernatural power. He thinks he's all that. People reinforce his misguided arrogance, calling him "the Great Power of God." Some people even follow Simon because of his amazing abilities.

But when Philip, likely Philip (3), shows up and tells everyone about Jesus, they believe and are baptized. Even Simon believes and is baptized too. He follows Philip everywhere, astonished by the godly supernatural power that Philip wields.

When the leaders in Jerusalem hear about Philip's work in Samaria, they send Peter and John to check things out. Once there, Peter and John place their hands on the believers, and they receive Holy Spirit power.

Simon is beside himself. He wants the ability to impart Holy Spirit power too. He offers to buy this skill. "I want to do this too. I can pay."

Peter is quick to condemn Simon. "You can't buy God's gift. Change your selfish ideas now. Pray that God will forgive you for this wickedness in you." Then Peter adds that he perceives Simon has a bitter heart and is a slave to evil.

Simon freaks out. "Please! Pray to God so that nothing bad happens to me."

But that's where the story ends. We don't know what happens next to Simon. Does he repent and correct his wrong thinking, or does he persist in trying to follow Jesus and be a sorcerer at the same time?

Do we ever try to mix wrong practices and beliefs along with our faith in Jesus?

[Discover more about Simon the Sorcerer in Acts 8:9–24.]

Saul (2)

S aul is a young Jew. He's also a Pharisee to the extreme, pursuing righteous actions with legalistic fervor. He kills in the name of his religion.

Saul sees Jesus's followers as a threat to his beliefs and the Jewish religious institution. When a Jewish mob stones Stephen, Saul stands as a witness, giving his approval. Stephen's death sends Jesus's followers scattering in all directions and sends Saul on a crusade to stop this growing movement. He seeks to imprison those who follow the Way of Jesus, even threatening to kill them.

Planning another string of arrests, Saul travels to Damascus with a group of friends.

On the way there, he encounters Jesus in the form of a heavenly flash of light and hears his voice from heaven. Jesus tells Saul to go to Damascus and wait for further instructions.

Saul's friends don't know what to say or think. Though they hear Jesus speak, they see nothing.

After he's blinded by the light, Saul's friends guide him to Damascus. He fasts for three days and prays. God sends a vision to Saul of a man, Ananias (2), coming to lay hands on him, so he can see again.

Ananias shows up and confirms that Saul did indeed encounter Jesus. Ananias heals Saul and fills him with the Holy Spirit.

In an instant Saul can see again. He's baptized and breaks his fast. Then he hangs out with Jesus's disciples in Damascus for several days. From now on Saul will follow Jesus.

What lengths will God go through to get our attention? Does he have to use drastic measures or are we open to listen?

[Discover more about Saul in Acts 7:58, Acts 8:3, Acts 9:1–19, Acts 22:3–20, and Philippians 3:4–6. Read part 2 of this story in the upcoming chapter about Paul.]

Ananias (2)

After the Jewish leaders martyr Stephen for his faith, the Pharisee Saul goes on a rampage. He seeks to arrest Jesus's followers and threatens to kill them. To avoid persecution, Jesus's squad scatters. Saul chases them. He goes to Damascus with authorization to seek out people who follow Jesus, both men and women, and drag them as prisoners back to Jerusalem.

On the way there, Saul encounters Jesus and is blinded as a result. Unable to see for three days, Saul fasts.

During this time, Jesus appears in a vision to the disciple Ananias. "Go find Saul, for he is praying. He's expecting you to come and heal him, so he can see again."

Ananias isn't so sure. "I've heard about this guy and all the damage he's caused to your people in Jerusalem. Now he's come here to do the same thing."

"Go!" God says. "It's all part of my plan."

Ananias goes, places his hands on Saul, and says, "Jesus who appeared to you on the road has sent me, so you can see again—and be filled with the Holy Spirit."

As if a blindfold is removed, Saul can see again. He gets up and is baptized.

Despite facing arrest and the possibility of execution if Saul captures him, Ananias obeys God and does what seems foolish.

Are we willing to risk death to obey what God tells us to do?

[Discover more about Ananias in Acts 9:10–19 and Acts 22:12.]

Tabitha (Dorcas)

Tabitha, also known as Dorcas, lives in Joppa. Luke says she's a disciple and a good person. She enjoys helping poor people. One way she does this is by making clothes for people in need.

She gets sick and dies.

Her friends prepare her body for burial. They mourn her death, while celebrating her life.

Peter's in a nearby town.

Some faith-filled followers of Jesus send for him. They ask him to come as soon as possible.

Peter agrees. When he arrives, he goes to where they've laid her body for viewing. He looks at her and tells her to get up.

She does.

Peter guides her to the balcony. He presents her to all those gathered to pay their respects. News of this amazing miracle spreads fast. As a result, many more people believe in Jesus.

Tabitha dedicates her life to helping people in need, but, like Jesus, it's her death and resurrection that helps them the most.

May both our life and our death point people to Jesus. What should we do to make sure this happens?

[Discover more about Tabitha in Acts 9:36–42.]

Cornelius

Cornelius emerges as a bit of an enigma.

On one hand he's part of the Roman military, a force known for its brutality and absolute power. He's part of this machine, a centurion with one hundred soldiers under his command.

Yet Cornelius is also a religious guy. His family is a devout, God-fearing clan. He helps those in need and prays often.

One day while in prayer, he has a supernatural vision. As clear as can be, he sees an angel from God who calls him by name.

Shocked and afraid, Cornelius answers, "What do you want Lord?"

The angel answers that God has heard Cornelius's prayers and received his gifts to the poor as a memorial offering. "Now send for Simon Peter. He's in Joppa staying at Simon the tanner's house by the sea." Then the angel disappears. Cornelius sends his staff and a soldier to fetch Peter.

The next day, Peter has a vision of his own. It's a bit confusing, commanding him to do something he was taught he should never do. The vision repeats two more times. As he's trying to make sense of this, Cornelius's delegation shows up. At the same time God's Spirit tells

Peter, "Three men are looking for you. I sent them. Go with them. Don't hesitate."

Peter goes.

His strange vision now makes sense. Though he was taught to not enter the home of a foreigner, God is turning things upside down. He will no longer favor the Jews, instead accepting all people who want to follow him.

Peter goes with Cornelius's messengers and enters his home, even though it's contrary to proper Jewish behavior. They hang out and talk about Jesus. As Peter speaks, the Holy Spirit comes upon Cornelius, his family, and his friends. Peter baptizes them in Jesus's name and spends a couple of days with them.

God is doing a new thing, providing salvation to all people.

How do we react when a new thing God does confronts our religious training or practices?

[Discover more about Cornelius in Acts 10.]

John Mark

We first read about John, also called Mark, in Acts. His mother's name is Mary (7). Jesus's followers are having a prayer meeting at her house, asking God to release Peter, who is in prison. John Mark doesn't play any role in the story, but the author of Acts feels it's important that we know he's present.

John Mark is a cousin of Barnabas. Barnabas wants to take John Mark with him and Saul (later called Paul) on one of their mission trips. Saul objects because John Mark had bailed on them in the past, but Barnabas sees potential in his cousin.

Saul and Barnabas debate the issue, but they can't reach a consensus. Their pointed dispute over John Mark causes them to end their partnership and go their separate ways. Though a sad development, this allows them to cover more territory and mentor other people. God turns their disagreement into something good.

Based on this event, we may assume Saul has no use for John Mark and writes him off. But this isn't true.

The two of them reconcile. We get a hint of this at the end of Saul's second letter to Timothy. There Saul instructs his protégé, "When you come, bring John Mark with you, for he's helpful to me in my work."

Furthermore, Saul notes that John Mark is with him when he writes to his friend Philemon.

Though John Mark initially proves himself unworthy, he turns things around and wins Saul's approval. Also, many scholars think that it's John Mark who writes the biography of Jesus that we call Mark.

When we flounder, do we give up or push through to turn things around?

[Discover more about John Mark in Acts 12:12, Acts 12:25, Acts 13:13, Acts 15:36–41, Colossians 4:10, 2 Timothy 4:11, Philemon 1:23–24, and 1 Peter 5:13. Though not all of these verses specify John Mark, the context makes it reasonable to conclude they're the same person.]

Rhoda

Rhoda is present at the prayer meeting for Peter when he's sitting in jail and facing execution. Rhoda is a servant, possibly of Mary (7) (mother of John Mark) at whose house the people have met to pray. We gather that Rhoda is also a follower of Jesus, praying for Peter along with everyone else.

During the prayer meeting, there's a knock on the door. As part of her duties, Rhoda goes to the door. Fearing for their safety, lest they're arrested too, she asks who's there. Peter identifies himself.

Overjoyed at hearing his voice, Rhoda runs to tell everyone the good news that Peter is there, but she forgets to let him in.

The people, despite their intense prayers for Peter's release, don't believe God answered their request. Though they pray for a miracle, they fear the worst. It's only after Peter's continued knocking that they let him in and discover the truth. Once they see him, they finally realize God's amazing answer to their prayers.

Unlike the others present, Rhoda prays with expectation. Merely hearing Peter's voice is all the evidence she needs. Everyone else doubts. Their faith may not be as strong as Rhoda's.

When we pray, do we pray in faith with expectation of answers or in doubt out of fear? Or is it okay for our prayers to have a mixture of belief and unbelief?

[Discover more about Rhoda in Acts 12:12–16.]

Paul

We've already covered the conversion of Saul (2) on the road to Damascus. Three days later, when Ananias (2) lays hands on Saul, he receives his sight and Holy Spirit power. Then Saul breaks his fast and is baptized. From there, he grows as a follower of Jesus. He begins traveling to tell others about Jesus, being used powerfully by God to do so.

As he journeys with Barnabas to Cyprus, we read a subtle shift in his name. Luke simply writes, "Saul, also called Paul." Though we don't know why Luke chooses this time to mark his change of names, we do see Saul transition to Paul, just as he had a faith transition from being a Pharisee to a follower of Jesus.

The name Saul appears twenty-nine times in the first part of the book of Acts, whereas the name Paul occurs 183 times in the remainder of the book and 239 times in the New Testament, altogether.

Paul goes on several missionary trips to tell people about Jesus. He starts churches in various cities, and mentors many people to move into leadership roles. In his travels he also suffers much for his faith. He's imprisoned, flogged, beaten, stoned, and shipwrecked, among other afflictions. Through all this, Paul presses on.

A prolific writer, Paul pens several letters to various churches and people. This is to encourage them and offer correction when needed. These make up about half the books of the New Testament and about one third of its content. Paul writes Romans, 1 Corinthians, 2 Corinthians, Galatians, Ephesians, Philippians, Colossians, 1 Thessalonians, 2 Thessalonians, 1 Timothy, 2 Timothy, Titus, and Philemon.

Toward the end of his life, Paul writes to his protégé Timothy. Paul says that he fought well, finished his race, and stayed true to his faith.

Despite many hardships and reasons to quit, Paul perseveres to the end.

What must we do to fight well, finish our race, and stay true to our faith?

[Discover more about Paul in Acts 13:9, 2 Corinthians 11:16–28, and 2 Timothy 4:7.]

Elymas (Bar-Jesus)

Barnabas and Paul/Saul sail to Cyprus and travel the island telling people about Jesus. When they get to Paphos, they meet Bar-Jesus, a Jewish sorcerer (in this case, a magician who practices witchcraft) and false prophet. His Greek name is Elymas.

He's also an aide to the Roman governor, Sergius Paulus. Sergius wants to learn more about Jesus, but Elymas opposes Barnabas and Paul and tries to thwart their influence over his boss.

Paul will have none of it. Filled with the Holy Spirit, he glares at Elymas. "You're the devil's spawn and the enemy of all that's good. You're full of lies and tricks. Why do you persist in perverting God's ways?" Then Paul adds the kicker: "God's had enough of you and will strike you blind."

At that moment, Elymas loses his sight. In a panic, he gropes around, seeking someone to take his hand and guide him.

This gets Sergius's attention. He's amazed and believes in Jesus.

But we don't know what happens to Elymas. Is his blindness temporary? Maybe Paul heals him. If so, does Paul heal him right away? Or maybe God, through Paul, is content to leave Elymas blind for a while. After all, when Paul first encountered Jesus, he remained blind for three days until Ananias (2), led by the Holy Spirit, healed Paul and restored his sight.

I'm glad that Sergius believes in Jesus, and I hope that Elymas will soon see again. But more importantly, I hope that Elymas will believe in Jesus too.

What might we unintentionally do to stand in the way of others who want to learn more about Jesus?

[Discover more about Elymas in Acts 13:6–12.]

Silas

When Paul and Barnabas end their missionary partnership, each one selects a new mentee and heads in different directions. Barnabas takes his cousin, John Mark, while Paul picks Silas.

But even before Paul picks Silas to mentor, Silas is a leader in the church. He was part of the special delegation to Antioch. The group carried an important message to squelch misinformation and give essential direction to that local church. Having already proven himself, it's not surprising that Paul picks Silas for his new missionary partner.

Paul and Silas travel to the various churches in the area to encourage and teach them. Among the places they go to are Philippi, Thessalonica, Berea, Athens, and Corinth. In Philippi they meet Lydia, the fortune-teller, and the Philippian jailer. We'll learn about them in upcoming chapters.

Later, Silas is with Paul (and Timothy) when Paul writes his two letters to the church in Thessalonica. But Silas doesn't just work with Paul, he also helps Peter. Peter affirms this in his second letter, where he regards Silas as a faithful brother.

We don't see Silas taking a lead role in any of this, but he does serve in a loyal support position to both Paul and Peter.

Are we willing to serve God if we can't play a lead role? God places us where he wants us, but do we do all we can to serve him in the best way possible?

[Discover more about Silas in Acts 15:22–Acts 18:5, 2 Corinthians 1:19, 1 Thessalonians 1:1, 2 Thessalonians 1:1, and 1 Peter 5:12.]

Timothy

Paul mentors many leaders in the church, and Timothy is one of them. Timothy later becomes a pastor, and Paul writes two letters of encouragement and instruction to him.

But we first encounter Timothy in the city of Lystra. He is a disciple of Jesus. And he has a mixed heritage. His mother, a Jew, is also a believer, but his father is Greek. Paul affirms Timothy's sincere faith, which started with his grandma Lois, moved to his mother Eunice, and now lives in him. What a godly legacy. The church in Lystra also speaks well of him.

Paul develops a real affinity for Timothy, referring to him as "a true son in the faith." Since there's nothing to indicate that Timothy's Greek father shares his faith, it's not surprising that Paul emerges as a father figure for the young man.

Throughout the book of Acts, we often see Timothy working in a key role as part of Paul's ministry. Paul calls him a coworker. Sometimes Timothy travels with Paul and other times Paul sends Timothy on special missions.

Timothy's name also pops up in Paul's two letters to the churches in Corinth and Thessalonica, as well as his letters to the Philippians, Colossians, and Philemon.

Timothy's inclusion in each of these letters confirm his role in helping the church grow and advance the cause of Jesus.

Is there someone we can mentor, just like Paul mentored Timothy?

[Discover more about Timothy in Acts 16:1–2, Acts 17:14–15, Acts 18:5, Acts 19:22, Romans 16:21, 1 Corinthians 4:17, 1 Timothy 1:1–5, and 2 Timothy 1:5.]

Lydia

Lydia is a merchant who sells expensive purple material. She lives in Philippi. She worships God but doesn't know about Jesus.

When Paul shows up, he tells her who Jesus is and what he did. She wants to follow Jesus too. She believes and is baptized to show her commitment to him. Then she asks Paul and his buddies to stay at her house.

Later, Paul and Silas heal a fortune-telling slave girl and end up in jail as a result. The next day they're released and head back to Lydia's where they meet with more of Jesus's followers. After encouraging them, Paul and Silas leave town.

When Lydia decides to follow Jesus, she goes all in. She even has people meet at her home. She doesn't need to take a class, join a church, or wait until her faith matures. She does what she can right away.

We later learn of an active local church in Philippi. I imagine Lydia is a key part of it. They might still meet at her house.

Do we make people wait before we let them serve Jesus or help at church?

[Discover more about Lydia in Acts 16:14–15 and Acts 16:40.]

The Fortune-Teller

When Paul and Silas are in Philippi, they meet a slave girl who has the psychic ability to tell people's future. Using her fortune-telling skills, she earns a great deal of money for her owners.

When she sees Paul, the spirit within her shouts supernatural truth: "These men are servants from God Most High. They're telling you how to get saved." She continues proclaiming this day after day. Finally, Paul grows exasperated. Evoking Jesus's name, Paul commands the fortune-telling spirit to leave her.

The spirit obeys, and the girl loses the ability to tell people their future. Her owners can no longer charge people for having her tell them their fortunes.

She's now free of her controlling spirit. Though we don't know what happens to her after this, we do know what happens to Paul and Silas: they spend a night in the pokey for their trouble.

The slave girl is exploited by her owners and spiritually freed by Jesus, through Paul's boldness.

Who does Jesus want us to help become free? He'll take the lead. All we need to do is follow.

[Discover more about this fortune-telling slave girl in Acts 16:16–19.]

The Philippian Jailer

After casting the fortune-telling spirit out of the slave girl, freeing her from possession in the spiritual realm and exploitation in the physical realm, Paul and Silas end up in trouble.

Though this is Paul's doing—when he commanded the spirit to come out of the fortune-teller—Silas is guilty by association. Dragged before the authorities, Paul and Silas are stripped, flogged, and thrown into prison.

Instead of feeling sorry for their predicament, they spend their time in jail praying and singing about God. They have a captive audience. All the other prisoners hear their impromptu concert. This goes on until midnight. I wonder if the prisoners are inspired by the praise music or angry about having their sleep interrupted.

Suddenly an earthquake shakes the prison, the doors fly open, and everyone's chains fall off. They're free!

The jailer awakes and assumes all his prisoners have escaped. He prepares to kill himself because he faces an even worse fate from his Roman boss. But Paul intervenes, "Wait, don't do it! We're still here."

The jailer calls for a torch, rushes to Paul and Silas, and falls before them, shaking in fear. He asks, "How can I get right with God?" Paul and Silas explain Jesus to him. After he treats their wounds, Paul and Silas baptize him and his family. Then, full of joy, he brings them into his home, and they share a meal.

The Philippian jailer made a wrong assumption and almost killed himself. Fortunately, he didn't, and was able to receive the saving goodness of Jesus.

Do we ever jump to the wrong conclusions and get in the way of what Jesus is trying to do?

[Discover more about the Philippian jailer in Acts 16:22–40.]

Jason

After Paul and Silas's encounter with Lydia, the fortune-teller, and the jailer, they leave Philippi and head for Thessalonica. As is Paul's practice, he heads to the local synagogue. For three Sabbaths, he tells the Jews about Jesus. Some decide to follow Jesus, including some God-fearing Greeks and women of influence.

But as is the case during a time of spiritual revival, not everyone is happy. Other Jews grow jealous of Paul and Silas's success in getting people to turn to Jesus. Instead of seeing God at work, they see this as opposition to their religious status quo. They must stop Paul and Silas before they lose any more of their followers and any more of their influence.

So what do they do?

They hire some slackers to form a mob and start a riot. Then the frenzied horde rushes into Jason's house looking for Paul and Silas. It's likely the local followers of Jesus were meeting in Jason's home, and the mob assumed Paul and Silas would be there.

Nonetheless, when the rioters can't find Paul or Silas, they grab Jason and the other believers who are there. They drag them before the authorities. There they make accusations against Team Jesus and condemn Jason for opening his home to them. They also charge the believers for opposing Roman rule by serving a different king—Jesus.

The city officials and the crowd freak out when they hear this, so they make Jason and the believers post bail before letting them go. Then, as soon as it gets dark, Paul and Silas sneak out of town.

Much later, as Paul wraps up his letter to the church in Rome, he adds greetings from Timothy, Lucius, Sosipater, and Jason. Assuming this is the same Jason, we see that despite his ordeal in Thessalonica, he continues to help Paul in his ministry.

Sometimes there's a risk for following Jesus. Are we willing to take those risks?

[Discover more about Jason in Acts 17:5–9 and Romans 16:21.]

Priscilla and Aquila

Exiled from Rome, Priscilla and her husband, Aquila, are missionaries who work with local churches and help other missionaries. Tentmakers, like Paul, they first meet him in Corinth where they work together. Later they travel to Syria and then to Ephesus. While Paul goes on, Priscilla and Aquila stay in Ephesus to help that church grow.

In Ephesus they meet Apollos. An educated man, he tells others about God with much zeal, but he only knows about the baptism of John. Priscilla and Aquila explain the full story of Jesus to him. Then Apollos goes out on his own to tell others about Jesus.

In his letters, Paul calls Priscilla and Aquila his co-workers, confirms they risked their lives for him, and affirms the church's appreciation for their work.

Later Priscilla and Aquila are back in Rome when Paul writes to that church, and they are with Timothy when Paul sends his second letter to the young preacher. However, when Paul writes again to the church in Corinth, Priscilla and Aquila are with him. At some point they start a house church, but the Bible doesn't tell us where.

The Bible always mentions Priscilla and Aquila together, never as individuals. They work as a team. That's how they can best help the church of Jesus grow.

What's interesting is that contrary to the cultural norm of listing the husband, Aquila, first and the wife second, Luke and Paul usually name Priscilla first and then Aquila. While we could assume this means Priscilla takes a lead role in their work, another understanding is that they are equal partners, with both Luke and Paul often mentioning Priscilla first to show her equality in ministry.

If we serve God with our spouse, do we work as equal partners, or does one lead and receive all the credit?

[Discover more about Priscilla and Aquila in Acts 18:1–3, 18:18–19, 18:24–26, Romans 16:3–4, 1 Corinthians 16:19, and 2 Timothy 4:19.]

Apollos

Apollos is a Jew from the city of Alexandria, but he later moved to Ephesus. Well-educated, Apollos has a deep knowledge of the Jewish Scriptures. He knows about God's ways, is a charismatic speaker, and teaches others. Though what he says is correct, he doesn't know the whole story. He only knows about John's baptism.

When Priscilla and Aquila hear Apollos speak, they're impressed. They invite him into their home to tell them Jesus's story, for whom John prepared the way.

Armed with this knowledge, Apollos wants to go to Acacia. The church in Ephesus encourages him to go. They write letters of introduction for him. When he arrives, he helps the believers there. He engages in public debate with Jewish opponents, using the Scriptures to prove that Jesus is the Messiah.

This is the last we hear directly about Apollos's work. However, in some of Paul's letters we get glimpses of how powerful and effective he is at spreading the good news of Jesus.

When Paul writes to the church in Corinth, he implies that Apollos's teaching is equal to his own and Peter's. The only problem is that people are aligning themselves with one of these three teachers—human, fallible leaders. Then Paul adds, "I plant the seed, Apollos waters it, but God makes it grow."

When God calls us to a task, are we ready to acknowledge his role in the outcome?

[Discover more about Apollos in Acts 18:23–28, 1 Corinthians 1:12, 1 Corinthians 3:4–6, 1 Corinthians 3:21–23, 1 Corinthians 4:6–7, 1 Corinthians 16:12, and Titus 3:13.]

Demetrius (1)

Paul travels to Ephesus to help the believers there and spread the word about Jesus. Paul stays there for a couple years. First, he preaches with boldness in the synagogue, and later he leads discussions in a lecture hall. Under God's power, Paul performs some amazing miracles.

As Paul prepares to leave Ephesus, a tradesman named Demetrius sparks some serious opposition. He's a silversmith who specializes in making silver shrines for Artemis, a local deity whose temple is in the city.

Demetrius opposes Paul, not because of theological disagreement (not really) but because of financial threat. Demetrius and the other craftsmen earn their living making things for the worship of Artemis. He fears that as people turn to Jesus, they'll stop buying Artemis-related products.

He gathers his fellow tradesmen together and makes a passionate plea for them to act. Even though he has a profit motive, he argues that Jesus's followers are discrediting Artemis and robbing her of her divinity. He stirs them into a riotous fervor.

The mob rampages, shouting, "Hail Artemis, god of the Ephesians!" Soon the whole city is in an uproar. They grab some of Paul's ministry team, Gaius and Aristarchus, when they can't find Paul. Then they push

Alexander forward to talk, but when he starts speaking, they realize he's a Jew and shout him down. The tumult continues for two hours.

Eventually the city clerk quiets the crowd. He appeases them by affirming Artemis's greatness, but he also confirms that Paul and the other believers haven't wronged Artemis. He tells Demetrius and his crew that if they have a grievance, they must address it through proper channels. Then he chastises the crowd for their riotous behavior and sends everyone home.

The Bible tells us nothing more about Demetrius's opposition to Jesus's followers, so we can assume this is where the story ends.

Demetrius masked his personal agenda in religious terms. How often do we do the same?

[Discover more about Demetrius in Acts 19:23–41.]

Gaius

John writes a letter to his dear friend Gaius. It's recorded for us in the Bible. This is likely the same Gaius grabbed by the riotous crowd in Ephesus.

He, along with Aristarchus, goes with Paul, traveling to tell others about Jesus. This makes Gaius a missionary.

John's letter to Gaius is a short message. It's a warm letter, full of encouragement and affirmation. John also reinforces some teaching with Gaius. Then John tacks on a short testimony about Demetrius (2). It seems Gaius knows Demetrius, or John anticipates the two of them will interact. John simply writes that everyone speaks well of Demetrius. It's important to John that Gaius knows this.

We get one more insight into Gaius as Paul wraps up his book to the Romans. He notes that Gaius sends greetings to the Roman followers of Jesus, making mention of Gaius's hospitality.

Paul has enjoyed Gaius's hospitable nature and so has the whole church. We don't know where this church is, but his hospitality is well-known in the area.

Gaius first travels as a missionary and later opens his home to other missionaries as they travel.

Are we known for our hospitality? If not, what should we do about it?

[Discover more about Gaius in Acts 19:29, Romans 16:23, and 3 John 1:1.]

Aristarchus

Aristarchus isn't a leading player in the early church, but his name comes up on five occasions. From these we see a man committed to advancing the cause of Jesus.

We first encounter Aristarchus in Ephesus, during the riot caused by Demetrius (1) and his followers. Unable to locate Paul, the mob grabs Gaius and Aristarchus simply because they're part of Paul's team. Aristarchus and Gaius escape harm, but surely it must be a couple of tense hours as they wonder what will happen to them.

We see these two men a bit later when Paul travels through Macedonia. Not only are Aristarchus and Gaius part of his squad, so too are Sopater, Secundus, Timothy, Tychicus, and Trophimus.

When Paul writes to his friend Philemon, Aristarchus is present and sends his greeting to Philemon. In this correspondence, Paul calls Aristarchus one of his "fellow workers," along with Mark, Demas, and Luke.

Much later in Paul's life, as a prisoner, he boards a ship headed for Rome. Aristarchus is with him. We don't know if Aristarchus is also a prisoner or merely there to support Paul. However, when Paul writes to the church in Colossae, he does refer to Aristarchus as a fellow prisoner.

Though we don't know much about him, Aristarchus is part of Paul's missionary team, is esteemed as a fellow missionary, and suffers in prison for the work he has done.

Like Aristarchus, are we content to play a supporting role in a greater ministry?

[Discover more about Aristarchus in Acts 19:29, Acts 20:4, Acts 27:2, Colossians 4:10, and Philemon 1:24.]

Tychicus

fter the riot in Ephesus, Paul travels to Macedonia. Luke lists the team who goes with Paul, or at least part of the team: Sopater, Aristarchus, Secundus, Gaius, Timothy, Tychicus, and Trophimus. We've already covered Timothy, Aristarchus, and Gaius. We know nothing about Sopater because this is the only verse he appears in, and we know little about Trophimus.

That leaves Tychicus.

Tychicus makes an appearance in five Bible verses. The first is in Acts, and the other four are in Paul's letters. From these we learn that Tychicus is a trusted member of Paul's team, someone Paul often dispatches as his representative.

Paul tells the church in Ephesus that Tychicus is a dear brother and faithful servant of God. Paul plans to send Tychicus to them to give a personal update with information that isn't in his letter.

When Paul writes to his protégé Timothy, he confirms that he sent Tychicus to Ephesus. However, in Paul's letter to his protégé Titus, he writes of his plan to send Tychicus (or Artemas) to fill in for Titus so he can come to visit Paul.

Tychicus, a beloved brother, faithful missionary, and servant of God, helps Paul be more effective in ministry, serving as his ambassador and messenger. These roles aren't big, but they are important.

Regardless of the size of our assignment, are we a faithful servant of God?

[Discover more about Tychicus in Acts 20:4, Ephesians 6:21, Colossians 4:7, 2 Timothy 4:12, and Titus 3:12.]

Ananias (3)

Ananias (3) is a high priest and part of the religious Council, the Sanhedrin. This is at a time when the Jewish religious leaders are doing their best to get rid of Paul, trying to silence him forever or at least remove his influence on their community.

Paul, a prisoner for his beliefs and for telling others about Jesus, is brought before the Council. Paul looks at them and declares, "I've been faithful to God and have a clear conscience, up to this very day."

At that moment Ananias orders someone near Paul to hit him in the mouth. We don't know if this is a mere slap or a punch.

Regardless, Paul reacts. "You hypocrite! You claim to judge me according to the law, but you violate it by commanding someone to strike me."

The people standing next to Paul inform him that he just insulted God's high priest.

Paul apologizes.

However, Ananias's position shouldn't matter. Right is right and wrong is wrong. What Ananias did was wrong. Without justification, he ordered that Paul be punished.

Being high priest doesn't give him the right to do that, but his position does give him the power, whether it's okay or not. And the people support him in this.

Despite whatever good qualities Ananias may have, he's a corrupt leader who uses his power to advance his personal agenda, opposing God's plan in the process.

Whether we have little power or much, do we abuse what power we have or use it to honor God in all things?

[Discover more about Ananias in Acts 23:1–5 and Acts 24:1.]

Felix

Felix is a Roman governor in Caesarea. His jurisdiction is the next stop for Paul and his legal ordeal as a prisoner for telling others about Jesus.

In response to a threat against Paul's life, a Roman centurion moves Paul from Jerusalem to the garrison in Caesarea. Felix leaves Paul behind bars until his accusers arrive to present their case.

Five days later Ananias (3) shows up, along with some of the other religious leaders and their attorney, Tertullus. Paul's trial is convened, and Tertullus presents their case. He gives misinformation and accuses Paul of various crimes, but he offers no proof, though the Jewish leaders who came with Tertullus agree with everything he says.

Next Paul presents his defense, but he doesn't dissuade Felix.

He could release Paul—since the charges brought against him have no merit—but instead Felix keeps him in jail, hoping for a bribe. Two years later, when Felix leaves his post as governor, Paul still languishes in prison.

How often does our love for money keep us from doing what is right?

[Discover more about Felix in Acts 23:25–24:27 and Acts 25:14.]

Drusilla

Drusilla is Felix's wife. She's Jewish. He isn't—or at least he doesn't act like it. Drusilla only shows up once in the Bible, and it's in the middle of the account about Governor Felix and the prisoner Paul.

Paul sits in prison under false charges and with a conspiracy to kill him hanging over his head. The jail is under the authority of Governor Felix.

Several days after hearing Paul's case and deciding not to issue a judgment, Felix and Drusilla visit with Paul. He tells them about Jesus. He teaches Felix and Drusilla about faith, righteousness, self-control, and the coming judgment.

Paul's words strike fear in Felix, but, as with the court case, Felix again delays making a decision. Paul languishes in jail for two years.

Though the Bible tells us Felix's reaction to Paul's teaching, we don't know what Drusilla thinks. Is she convicted? Does she decide to believe in Jesus? Or is she unaffected by Paul's words?

However, we know that spouses can influence each other. Drusilla could have encouraged her husband to do the right thing and release Paul. She also could have urged him to act on Paul's teaching and follow Jesus.

Though we don't know if she tries either of these, we do know Felix doesn't let Paul go. We also know that Felix doesn't decide to follow Jesus.

Drusilla may have been able to change either one of these situations and influence Felix to act.

Are we doing all we can to inspire others to act justly and to follow Jesus?

[Discover more about Drusilla in Acts 24:24–27.]

Festus

After Felix lets Paul languish in jail for two years, he's replaced as governor by Porcius Festus. Shortly after he takes over, the Jewish leaders, not content to merely let Paul rot in prison, request that Festus transfer Paul back to Jerusalem. They're still plotting to ambush him along the way and kill him.

Instead, Festus tells them to come to Caesarea and present their case there. He convenes court and Paul's enemies accuse him of many serious charges, but they can't prove a thing. As for his part, Paul persists in claiming his innocence.

Confused by their accusations against Paul, Festus isn't sure how to proceed, so he asks if Paul will travel to Jerusalem to stand trial before the religious Council. Paul suspects a plot to kill him. To avoid returning to Jerusalem, he appeals his case to Caesar, a right he has as a Roman citizen.

Festus agrees with Paul's request. However, Festus doesn't know what charges to list in Paul's appeal to Caesar. King Agrippa and Bernice, who have a better understanding of the background of this situation, agree to give their input.

Paul makes his case before the three of them, and they conclude that Paul is innocent and could have been released, had he not appealed his case to Caesar.

How do we react when others face injustice?

[Discover more about Felix in Acts 24:27–26:32.]

King Agrippa and Bernice

Whenever we read of Bernice in the Bible it's in context with King Agrippa. They enter our story to determine the fate of the imprisoned Paul when Festus is unable to comprehend the situation or make an accurate determination. Though Agrippa takes the lead in this, throughout the story we see Bernice as a partner to him. She accompanies him to events, sits in on Paul's hearing, and is part of the follow-up meeting.

After hearing Paul present his case, they adjourn to discuss Paul's situation. Bernice takes part in reaching the group's conclusion that Paul hasn't done anything to deserve the severe penalty his detractors seek. Together, King Agrippa and Bernice make the right determination.

Whether a spouse, relative, or friend, God puts people in our lives to help us, support us, and encourage us. They can help us make wise decisions.

In the same way, God gives us opportunities to help, support, and encourage others. We can likewise guide them to make wise decisions.

Are we doing all we can to help those around us? Do we listen to the guidance of people God places in our lives?

[Discover more about King Agrippa and Bernice in Acts 25:13–26:32.]

Part 5:

———❧———

The Early Church Beyond Acts

I n the last section of *The Friends and Foes of Jesus*, we'll look at his followers and their opponents who aren't covered in the book of Acts. Though Luke doesn't document what these people do, they, too, move forward to organize (or oppose) Jesus's followers and teach them about what it is to be his disciples. Through them we learn more about the church of Jesus and encounter more diverse settings and interesting situations.

Phoebe

Paul wraps up his letter to the Romans by mentioning a string of people, several of them women. First up is Phoebe, a church deacon whom Paul commends and sends to Rome as a missionary. He tells the people there to assist her in every way possible. Paul ends by affirming that she has helped many other people, including himself.

For those who think women can't serve in church leadership or as a lone missionary, Phoebe's example shows us it wasn't always this way, especially in the beginning. Paul's affirmation of her confirms he doesn't place restrictions on how a woman can serve God.

Through the example of Phoebe, the Bible shows us that women can serve as deacons, as well as missionaries. Some churches cling to the belief that women can't be deacons (or elders), and some missionary agencies won't send a single woman into the field. But they ignore the precedent set by Phoebe in the Bible.

Furthermore, Paul tells the church in Rome to accept her and the work she's doing. Paul lauds Phoebe as a deacon, a missionary, and a huge help to the church of Jesus. Her gender doesn't matter.

How can Phoebe's example encourage us? Do we need to change our opinions about how women can serve God and his church?

[Discover more about Phoebe in Romans 16:1–2.]

Titus

We don't hear anything about Titus in the book of Acts. However, Titus receives multiple mentions in some of Paul's letters, especially in his second letter to the church in Corinth. Throughout these letters we see Titus as working with Paul to tell others about Jesus.

Though sometimes Paul and Titus work together, more often Paul sends Titus to various cities. Paul also writes a letter to Titus, whom he left in Crete to help build the church there. Another time, Paul sends Titus to Dalmatia.

In Paul's letter to the church in Galatia, we learn that Titus goes with Paul and Barnabas on a trip to Jerusalem. An interesting side note is that Titus, with Greek heritage and not being circumcised, isn't forced to undergo this Jewish tradition, which contrasts with Timothy, whom Paul does circumcise. Does the view of circumcision change or is it dependent on individual factors?

One time in Paul's travels, he goes to Troas to preach because God provides an opportunity for him to do so, but he has no peace because he can't find Titus. So Paul leaves for Macedonia. It's in Macedonia that Titus provides Paul and his team with much comfort during a discouraging situation.

This is, in part, because Titus's spirit has just been refreshed from his visit to the church in Corinth. It's in Paul's second letter to them that he calls Titus his partner and coworker. This is a fitting tribute to the important work of Titus in advancing the kingdom of Jesus.

Are we a partner and coworker with those who advance Jesus's kingdom?

[Discover more about Titus in 2 Corinthians 2:12–13, 2 Corinthians 7:6–7, 2 Corinthians 7:13–15, 2 Corinthians 8:6–24, 2 Corinthians 12:18, Galatians 2:1–3, 2 Timothy 4:10, and Titus 1:4–5.]

Euodia and Syntyche

Euodia and Syntyche are two women who work hard for Team Jesus. Paul calls them his coworkers, for they struggle at his side to spread the good news about Jesus. Their actions are commendable, and it would be great to celebrate their diligent labor.

However, another trait—an unfortunate one—overshadows their work to advance God's kingdom. They can't get along. Though they share a common goal, they live in disharmony with each other. They disagree. They fight. They argue.

Each one thinks she is right and the other, wrong. Both have too much pride to back down. Their interpersonal struggle affects those around them. They hurt the common cause they work so hard to advance. Their bickering harms the church of Jesus.

Even though he isn't present, Paul acts.

He begs them to get along, work through their spat, and put it behind them. Notice that Paul doesn't take sides or try to mediate their dispute. He just tells them to get along and stop arguing. Do they listen and do as Paul asks?

The work of God is important. However, despite our best efforts, we sometimes get in the way, thwarting the effectiveness of our labor through petty squabbles and ungodly behavior.

Are we to be commended for our work or criticized for arguing about unimportant issues?

[Discover more about Euodia and Syntyche in Philippians 4:2–3.]

Epaphras

A nother associate of Paul's is Epaphras. We don't know much about him. His name only appears three times in the Bible, all of which are in two of Paul's letters: one to the church in Colossae and the other to his friend Philemon. Yet, packed in these three verses is much insight into the godly character of Epaphras.

We learn that Epaphras is from Colossae. He teaches the people there about Jesus and encourages them to grow in their faith.

Paul affirms Epaphras as a cherished servant and faithful minister of Jesus, part of Paul's squad. These are both significant characteristics, but there's more.

Epaphras is also a prayer warrior for his people. Paul notes that Epaphras wrestles in prayer for them. His prayers aren't just occasionally or often, but Paul says that Epaphras *always* prays for them. He prays to God that the church in Colossae will stand firm, obey God's will, and be mature and fully assured in their faith.

Not only does Epaphras work hard for the church in Colossae but also for the churches in Laodicea and Hierapolis.

Epaphras is a beloved servant, faithful minister, and committed prayer warrior. May we follow his example.

What would it take for us to be a prayer warrior? And if always being in prayer isn't our thing, what else can we do to serve God and advance his kingdom?

[Discover more about Epaphras in Colossians 1:6–8, Colossians 4:12–13, and Philemon 1:23–24.]

Demas

Demas is another associate of Paul. The Bible mentions Demas three times, which gives us some insight into him.

First, we know Demas is with Paul when he writes to the church in Colossae. This is because Demas, along with Luke, sends their greetings to the Colossian church in this letter.

Similarly, in Paul's letter to his friend Philemon, Demas is among four people who send greetings. In addition to Demas, we have Aristarchus, Mark, and Luke. Paul affirms all four as his fellow workers.

The third mention of Demas is in Paul's second letter to his protégé Timothy. In this instance, the reference to Demas is sad. Paul is overwhelmed because most of his support group is gone. He has dispatched Crescens to Galatia and Titus to Dalmatia. Only Luke remains. This is because Demas deserted Paul and took off for Thessalonica.

However, we don't know the chronological order of these three events, and Bible scholars can only speculate as to when Paul wrote each letter.

If Paul writes to Philemon before he writes to Timothy, then we see Demas, who was once a fellow worker of Paul, desert him later. However, if we consider these in the opposite order, we see Demas leaving Paul and later being reconciled to him, earning the status of being called a fellow worker.

The optimist in me hopes that Demas ends well, as a fellow worker of Paul. The pessimist in me fears that in his last action, Demas lets Paul down and brings about one of Paul's darkest moments.

Yet regardless of Demas's actions and our actions, Jesus still loves us, offering us his grace and mercy.

When we mess up, like Demas did, will we allow it to define us or seek God's grace and mercy to restore us into a right relationship with him?

[Discover more about Demas in Colossians 4:14, 2 Timothy 4:9–10, and Philemon 1:23–24.]

Onesiphorus

Onesiphorus is another obscure character in the New Testament. We only hear of him twice, and both times it's in Paul's second letter to his protégé Timothy.

In the opening chapter, Paul writes a prayer of blessing for Onesiphorus—asking God to show mercy to his household. There's a reason Paul makes this request. It's because Onesiphorus has often encouraged Paul and wasn't embarrassed to meet with him in prison.

Paul goes on to say that when he was in Rome, likely in jail, Onesiphorus made a diligent search until he found him. That's dedication and determination. Then, after another prayer request that God will grant that Onesiphorus find mercy, Paul also affirms the many ways Onesiphorus helped him in Ephesus.

Later, as Paul wraps up his letter to Timothy, Paul tells him to greet Priscilla, Aquila, and the household of Onesiphorus. This is interesting. Both times we read of Onesiphorus, it's in conjunction with his household. This would include his family and possibly servants.

Why does Paul mention Onesiphorus's household? Perhaps he leads a large, noteworthy clan. Or maybe his family is giving him grief, so Paul knows Onesiphorus needs encouragement. These are conjectures. In truth we don't know.

Peter DeHaan, PhD

What we do know is how Onesiphorus encourages Paul, visits him in jail, and diligently searches for him. As a result, Onesiphorus earns Paul's appreciation and his prayers, for both him and his household.

When we pray for others, do we also pray for their household? Should we?

[Discover more about Onesiphorus in 2 Timothy 1:16–18 and 2 Timothy 4:19.]

198

Claudia

As Paul wraps up his second letter to his protégé Timothy, some of Paul's associates add their greetings to his message. First there is Eubulus and then Pudens, followed by Linus. The fourth person, Claudia, is the only female in the group. But at least she's listed, because following her name comes a general greeting from everybody else. This is the only verse any of these four people appear in, so we know nothing else about them.

They likely play a critical role in the missionary work Paul leads. He recognizes their efforts by including their names in his letter, which is preserved for us to read today. Is Claudia honored to be listed or is she disappointed to appear fourth, even though others aren't mentioned at all?

Sometimes, like Claudia, we receive public recognition for the work we do. Other times we're identified indirectly as part of a team. Sometimes we receive no acknowledgment for our efforts at all.

From a human perspective, this matters a lot. Would we become proud for being listed, mad that we weren't mentioned first, or angry that we received only a generic nod or no acknowledgment at all?

God's perspective is quite different. He desires that we work for him. Not for an earthly reward—be it money, fame, or recognition—but for a heavenly one. Our reward will occur later when he says, "Well done! You're a good and faithful servant." And that should be enough.

Do we sometimes do godly things for human rewards? Do we feel slighted when no one acknowledges us?

[Discover more about Claudia in 2 Timothy 4:21. Read about receiving affirmation for being a good and faithful servant in Matthew 25:21.]

Philemon

The name Philemon only appears once in the Bible. It's in the letter from Paul to his friend. We refer to this letter by the name of its recipient: Philemon.

Paul opens his letter affirming Philemon's actions and character.

Then Paul gets to the purpose of his letter. It's a big ask.

It seems Philemon is well-off: the church meets in his home, and he owns slaves. One of his slaves is Onesimus. Onesimus runs away, meets Paul—who tells him about Jesus, and becomes a believer.

Paul desires to see Onesimus and Philemon's estranged relationship made right—because of Jesus. Paul encourages both to do the right thing: for Onesimus to return to his master regardless of the risk of punishment and for Philemon to welcome him back without penalty.

Reconciliation is the reason Paul writes his letter to Philemon. In doing so, Paul doesn't address the issue of slavery. Instead he focuses on the restoration of a relationship.

Paul can assume this role of reconciler because he has a personal connection with both parties. This history gives him a credibility that an outsider would have lacked, allowing him to positively influence them both.

Though we don't know if Onesimus is restored into right relationship with Philemon, given the strong emotional appeal Paul makes and his logic that supports it, we have good reason to expect a joyous reunion.

Has God put us in a position to reconcile an estranged relationship? What should we do about it?

[Discover more about Philemon in Philemon 1:1–25.]

Archippus

Archippus pops up twice in the Bible, both times in letters from Paul. The first is in Paul's message to his friend Philemon. In addition to Philemon, Archippus (along with Apphia) is listed as a recipient of the note. Though the letter is mainly to Philemon, for some reason Archippus is also included. The message must be relevant to him as well. He may be a leader in the church that meets in Philemon's home. Regardless of the reason, after listing Archippus, Paul affirms him as a colleague, a fellow soldier in the cause of Jesus.

Then in Paul's letter to the church in Colossae, he adds a personal message to Archippus. It's a seemingly random insertion as Paul wraps up his communication. Paul encourages Archippus to be sure to finish the work God gave him to do. We don't know what this job is, but we do see that Paul feels it's important to encourage Archippus to not leave things undone.

Over the years, many people have enthusiastically told me that God called them to do something for him. Yet when I run into them later, I learn they never followed through. Distractions, life, and their preconceived ideas get in the way. They may even question if they correctly heard God.

When God calls us to a task, we must complete it. We must be faithful to his request. Inaction is not an option.

What has God called us to do that we must strive to complete?

[Discover more about Archippus in Colossians 4:17 and Philemon 1:1–3.]

Onesimus

The focus of Paul's letter to Philemon is Onesimus, the runaway slave. Ironically, Onesimus means *useful*. An escaped slave isn't too useful to his master.

After Onesimus flees, he encounters Jesus through Paul. Paul mentors Onesimus and the two begin working together. However, it isn't right for Onesimus to remain with Paul—even though what they're doing is important. To do so would defraud Philemon of Onesimus's labor.

Paul encourages Onesimus to return to his master, despite the risk it involves. A recaptured slave could be punished. To facilitate a positive reunion, Paul writes a letter to Philemon, pleading for him to offer Onesimus mercy.

While we don't explicitly know the outcome of this drama, we can reasonably deduce it.

First, Paul's petition on Onesimus's behalf is so powerful that it's hard to imagine anyone not complying.

Second, in the only other mention of Onesimus in the Bible, Paul announces he is sending Tychicus and Onesimus to the people of Colossae. Paul also affirms Onesimus as a faithful and dear brother. Since this trip could not have reasonably occurred prior to Onesimus returning to Philemon, we can assume that Philemon did as Paul requested, allowing Onesimus to return to Paul to work with him on Philemon's behalf. This would put Onesimus in a position to take that trip to Colossae.

At last Onesimus can be useful, to both Paul and Philemon, as well as to the Colossians and to God. This all happens because Onesimus does the right thing, returning to his master despite the risk.

Do we do the right thing regardless of the cost?

[Discover more about Onesimus in Philemon 1:8–21.]

Demetrius (2)

Luke writes about Demetrius (1), the silversmith, who opposes Paul and the followers of Jesus.

But John writes about a different Demetrius, Demetrius (2), one highly esteemed. This occurs in John's letter to his dear friend Gaius. The letter is a short message full of encouragement, affirmation, and teaching. Then, inserted into the letter are two seemingly random and obscure sentences about Demetrius. Apparently Gaius knows Demetrius. Or maybe John anticipates the two of them will one day meet.

Of Demetrius, John simply writes, "Everyone speaks well of him." Then John adds, "We do too, and we don't lie."

We don't know why John feels it's important to communicate this truth about Demetrius to Gaius. Even more so, we're left to speculate why Demetrius is so highly esteemed. He must be a man of noble character and impeccable integrity.

Regardless, Demetrius is an example for us to emulate. For when we are well-spoken-of by everyone, we most effectively represent Jesus to them.

Do people speak well of us? If not, what should we do to change that?

[Discover more about Demetrius in 3 John 1:12.]

Diotrephes

In John's letter to his friend Gaius, he not only mentions Demetrius, whom everyone respects, but he also names Diotrephes. Unfortunately, Diotrephes is not so highly esteemed. This guy has issues. He's a control freak.

To start with, Diotrephes loves to be first. He wants to be in charge.

At one time, John wrote a letter to the local church Diotrephes is part of, but he refused to accept what John said. On John's next visit he promises to publicly call out Diotrephes's inappropriate actions.

In addition to loving to be first and not accepting John's message, Diotrephes compounds the problem by gossiping about John and other disciples. Diotrephes's smear campaign promotes spiteful rumors. It must stop.

Not only does Diotrephes refuse to welcome John and his crew, he also refuses to welcome other believers when they visit. But this isn't only a personal attack. He also stops others in the church from welcoming visitors and kicks them out if they try.

Diotrephes is part of Jesus's church, but his actions certainly don't honor Jesus or support his followers. Diotrephes serves as internal opposition to Jesus. He is a foe of Jesus from within the church.

Do we ever seek to be in control? Do we love to be first? If so, what do we need to change to honor Jesus and support his church?

[Discover more about Diotrephes in 3 John 1:9–10.]

Jude

Jude is another name that only appears once in the Bible. It's the first word in the opening sentence of the letter that bears his name. Though the introduction gives hints as to who Jude is, no one knows for sure. Jude calls himself a servant of Jesus and a brother of James. One speculation is that Jude is a nickname for Judas, which could make him, along with James, a half-brother to Jesus.

Regardless of who Jude is, he writes a generic letter, not to a church or an individual, but to all who follow Jesus. He blesses them with abundant mercy, peace, and love.

Though he planned to write about their common salvation, instead he writes to encourage them to contend for their faith.

Why is this? Because ungodly people have slipped into Jesus's church.

What are they doing? They're turning God's grace (undeserved favor) into an excuse to act immorally. They claim they can behave however they wish because God will forgive them. Though immorality covers a range of improper behaviors, it especially refers to sexual issues. In short, these people act out sexually because they claim what they do doesn't matter.

In addition to their sexual depravity, they also deny that Jesus is their Savior. How they can do this and still assume he'll forgive them doesn't make sense. But they advocate it just the same. To combat this, Jude reminds his friends about the past, urging them to persevere in standing true to their faith in God.

We must guard against improper sexual behavior in the church. And we must guard against people who claim Jesus isn't the way to salvation.

Where do we draw the line between accepting those who believe differently than we do and standing up against people who try to corrupt our faith?

[Discover more about Jude in Jude 1:1–25.]

Jezebel (2)

The church in Thyatira has a problem. It's not a thing but a person. Her name is Jezebel.

Though she calls herself a prophet, she misleads people. That makes her a bad prophet. She encourages the church to engage in immoral behavior and unholy actions. She even advocates Satanism. Not only does Jesus promise a harsh punishment to her and her followers, he also criticizes those who tolerate her, by allowing her errant teaching to go unchecked.

Tolerance of others is usually a good thing. But sometimes tolerance is unacceptable, such as in the face of wrong teaching that encourages people to sin or leads them away from Jesus.

This doesn't apply to differences of opinion or theological disputes. Those instances do demand tolerance. Acceptance is key. Love, in the name of Jesus, is the standard.

However, we must speak against people who try to pull others away from Jesus, those who cause his followers to stumble in their faith.

May we never discourage others from pursuing God, and may we never tolerate those who would pull Jesus's followers away from him.

Are we ever tolerant when we shouldn't be? Are we ever intolerant when we should love?

[Discover more about Jezebel in Revelation 2:18–29. Learn what Jesus has to say about those who cause his followers to stumble in Luke 17:1–2.]

For Small Groups

*T*he *Friends and Foes of Jesus* makes an ideal discussion guide for small groups, Sunday School, or Bible classes. In preparation for your meeting, read one chapter of this book each day.

Then, when you get together in your small group, discuss the questions at the end of each chapter. The leader can guide this discussion for all the questions or pick certain ones to focus on.

Before beginning your discussion, pray as a group. Ask for Holy Spirit insight and clarity.

Then, while considering each chapter's question:

- Look for how this can grow our understanding of the Bible.
- Evaluate how this can expand our faith perspective.
- Consider what we need to change in how we live our lives.

End by asking God to help us apply what we've learned.

If you discussed *The Friends and Foes of Jesus* in a small group, Sunday School class, or a classroom, Peter would love to follow up with your group via Skype. Email his administrative assistant at author@PeterDeHaan.com to check his availability.

Bonus Content 1:

———∼∼∼———

Duplicate Names

Names often recur throughout the Bible, referring to different people from different eras or different situations. Here are the names covered in this book that also reference other people in the Bible. Some of these names are in both the Old and New Testaments, while others appear only in the New Testament. For each name, they are listed in approximate chronological order, with a number added to help us better identify them.

Ananias

Ananias (1), who, with his wife, Sapphira, tried to defraud God (Acts 5:1–6)

Ananias (2), who restores Saul's sight (Acts 9:10–19 and Acts 22:12)

Ananias (3), the High Priest (Acts 23:2 and Acts 24:1)

Barsabbas

Barsabbas (1), also called Joseph (7), as well as Justus, the man not picked to replace Judas (Acts 1:23–26)

Barsabbas (2), though this could be the same as Barsabbas (1), it's likely someone different because his other name is Judas (6) (Acts 15:22)

Centurion

Centurion (1), who in great faith asks Jesus to heal his servant (Matthew 8:5–13 and Luke 7:1–10)

Centurion (2), who witnesses Jesus's death (Matthew 27:54, Mark 15:39, Mark 15:44–45, and Luke 23:47)

Centurion (3), Cornelius (Acts 10:1–11 and Acts 10:24–48)

Centurion (4), who was about to flog Paul (Acts 22:25–26)

Centurion (5), who takes Paul's nephew to the commander with information (Acts 23:17–18)

Centurion (6), who will protect Paul (Acts 23:23)

Centurion (7), in charge of guarding Paul (Acts 24:23)

Centurion (8), Julius (Acts 27:1–43)

[Notes on Centurion: Centurion is a title, not a name. It's for a leader in the Roman army who oversees one hundred soldiers. Though it's possible some of these centurions could refer to the same person, it's likely each one is different, given the number of centurions that the Romans would have in the area at any given time.]

Demetrius

Demetrius (1), the silversmith (Acts 19:23–41)

Demetrius (2), highly esteemed (3 John 1:12)

Gamaliel

Gamaliel (1), son of Pedahzur (Numbers 1:10, Numbers 2:20, Numbers 7:54–59)

Gamaliel (2), a teacher of the Law and mentor to Saul/Paul (Acts 5:33–42 and Acts 22:3)

Herod

Herod (1), King Herod, also known as Herod the Great, who killed all the baby boys in Bethlehem (Matthew 2:1–20 and Luke 1:1)

Herod (2), the tetrarch, son of Herod the Great, who played a part in Jesus's execution (Matthew 14:1–12, Mark 6:14–28, and Luke 23:6–15)

Herod (3), historically, the grandson of Herod the Great (Acts 12:19–23)

James

James (1), a disciple, brother of John, and son of Zebedee (Matthew 4:21)

James (2), a disciple, and son of Alphaeus (Matthew 10:3, Mark 3:18, and Luke 6:15)

James (3), a half-brother of Jesus, and the likely author of the book of James (Matthew 13:55)

James (4), the father of Judas—though not Judas Iscariot (Luke 6:16)

James (5), "the younger," and son of Mary (4)—though he could be James (3) (Mark 15:40)

John

John (1) the Baptist, who King Herod (2) beheaded (Luke 9:9)

John (2), one of Jesus's twelve disciples (Matthew 10:2–4)

John (3), father of Simon Peter (John 21:15)

John (4), a member of Annas's family (Acts 4:6)

John (5), also known as John Mark or just Mark (Acts 12:25)

Joseph

Joseph (1), the son of Jacob, who was sold as a slave and ended up in Egypt (Genesis 37:2)

Joseph (2), son of Asaph (1 Chronicles 25:2)

Joseph (3), a priest guilty of marrying a foreign wife and a descendant of Binnui (Ezra 10:38–42 and possibly Nehemiah 12:14)

Joseph (4), stepfather of Jesus (Matthew 1:16)

Joseph (5), a half-brother of Jesus (Mark 6:3)

Joseph (6) of Arimathea, a disciple of Jesus and a member of the Council, who buried Jesus (Matthew 27:57)

Joseph (7) or Barsabbas, also known as Justus (Acts 1:23)

Joseph (8), a Levite from Cyprus, whom the apostles called Barnabas (Acts 4:36)

Judas

Judas (1) Iscariot, one of the twelve disciples. He later betrayed Jesus (Matthew 10:2–4)

Judas (2), a half-brother of Jesus (Matthew 13:55)

Judas (3), the son of James (Acts 1:13)

Judas (4), a Galilean and rebel leader (Acts 5:37)

Judas (5), who lives on Straight Street (Acts 9:11)

Judas (6), also called Barsabbas and an esteemed person in the early church (Acts 15:22)

Lazarus

Lazarus (1), the brother of Martha and Mary (3) whom Jesus raised from the dead (John 11:1–44)

Lazarus (2), a character in Jesus's parable about a rich man and a beggar named Lazarus (Luke 16:19–31)

Levi

Levi (1), one of Jacob's twelve sons (Genesis 29:34)

Levi (2), father of Kohath (Numbers 16:1)

Levi (3), an ancestor of Jesus, who is the father of Matthat (1) and son of Melki (Luke 3:24)

Levi (4), another ancestor of Jesus, who is the father of Matthat (2) and son of Simeon (Luke 3:29–30)

Levi (5), also known as Matthew and a tax collector who became a disciple of Jesus (Matthew 9:9)

Mary

Mary (1), mother of Jesus (Matthew 1:16)

Mary (2), Magdalene (Luke 8:2)

Mary (3), Martha and Lazarus's sister (Luke 10:38–42 and John 12:2–7)

Mary (4), the mother of James and Joseph (Matthew 27:55–56, Mark 15:40–41, Mark 16:1, and Luke 24:1–11)

Mary (5), the wife of Clopas (John 19:25)

Mary (6), the "other Mary" (Matthew 27:61 and Matthew 28:1)

Mary (7), the mother of John Mark (Acts 12:12–16)

Mary (8), a hard worker and associate of Paul (Romans 16:6)

[Read more about all eight Marys in *Women of the Bible*.]

Philip

Philip (1), one of Jesus's twelve disciples (Matthew 10:2–4)

Philip (2), brother of King Herod (2) and the first husband of Herodias (Mark 6:17)

Philip (3), deacon and evangelist (Acts 6:2–5, Acts 8:4–40, and Acts 21:8–9)

Saul

Saul (1) the first king of Israel (1 Samuel 10:1)

Saul (2), a young Pharisee who initially opposed Jesus's followers and was later called Paul (Acts 7:58, Acts 8:3, and Acts 9:1–19)

Simeon

Simeon (1), son of Jacob and Leah (Genesis 29:33)

Simeon (2), who anticipated the birth of Jesus (Luke 2:25–35)

Simeon (3), a prophet and teacher in Antioch, also called Niger (Acts 13:1)

Simon

Simon (1), a disciple, also call Peter, as in Simon Peter (Matthew 4:18)

Simon (2), the Zealot and another disciple (Matthew 10:4)

Simon (3), a half-brother of Jesus (Matthew 13:55)

Simon (4), the leper and the owner of the home where Jesus's head was anointed with oil (Mark 14:3)

Simon (5), a Pharisee and owner of the home where Jesus's feet were washed with perfume, though this could arguably be Simon (4) (Luke 7:39–50)

Simon (6), from Cyrene and who carried Jesus's cross (Luke 23:26)

Simon (7) Iscariot, father of Judas Iscariot (John 13:2)

Simon (8), the sorcerer who asked to buy Holy Spirit power (Acts 8:9–25)

Simon (9), the tanner, who Peter stayed with in Joppa when Cornelius sent for him (Acts 10:32)

Zechariah

Zechariah (1), king of Israel (2 Kings 14:29)

Zechariah (2), a descendant of Reuben (1 Chronicles 5:7–8)

Zechariah (3), the gatekeeper and son of Meshelemiah (1 Chronicles 9:21 and 1 Chronicles 26:1–2)

Zechariah (4), a descendant of Saul (1 Chronicles 9:37 and possibly 1 Chronicles 15:18)

Zechariah (5), a musician (1 Chronicles 15:20)

Zechariah (6), a priest (1 Chronicles 15:24)

Zechariah (7), a Levite during the time of King David (1 Chronicles 16:5)

Zechariah (8), another gatekeeper and son of Hosah (1 Chronicles 26:10–11)

Zechariah (9), a third gatekeeper, a wise counselor, and son of Shelemiah (1 Chronicles 26:14)

Zechariah (10), father of Iddo during the time of King David (1 Chronicles 27:21)

Zechariah (11), an official of King Jehoshaphat (2 Chronicles 17:7) and possibly his son (2 Chronicles 21:2)

Zechariah (12), son of Jehoiada the priest (2 Chronicles 24:20)

Zechariah (13), father of Abijah (2 Chronicles 29:1)

Zechariah (14), an official of King Josiah (2 Chronicles 35:8)

Zechariah (15), the prophet and a descendant of Iddo (Ezra 5:1, the book of Zechariah, and possibly Ezra 8:3)

Zechariah (16), a priest guilty of marrying a foreign woman (Ezra 10:18, 26)

Zechariah (17), son of Amariah and father of Uzziah (Nehemiah 11:4)

Zechariah (18), father of Joiarib and descendant of Zechariah (16) (Nehemiah 11:5)

Zechariah (19), son of Jonathan (Nehemiah 12:35)

Zechariah (20), a reliable witness and son of Jeberekiah (Isaiah 8:2)

Zechariah (21), son of Berekiah, who was murdered between the temple and the altar (Matthew 23:35)

Zechariah (22), the husband of Elizabeth and father of John the Baptist (Luke 1:5–25 and Luke 1:57–66)

[Note on Zechariah: With the number of obscure mentions of Zechariah throughout the Bible—fifty-nine times in nine books—it's impossible to accurately determine how many there are, but there are many. The main ones are Zechariah (1), king of Israel; Zechariah (15), the prophet; and Zechariah (22), father of John the Baptist. This listing is reasonable but not absolute.]

Bonus Content 2:

If You're New to the Bible

Each entry in this book has Bible references. These can guide you if you want to learn more. If you're not familiar with the Bible, here's a brief overview to get you started, give some context, and minimize confusion.

First, the Bible is a collection of works written by various authors over several centuries. Think of the Bible as a diverse anthology of godly communication. It has historical accounts, poetry, songs, letters of instruction and encouragement, messages from God sent through his representatives, and prophecies.

Most versions of the Bible have sixty-six books grouped into two sections: The Old Testament and the New Testament. The Old Testament has thirty-nine books that precede and anticipate Jesus. The New Testament includes twenty-seven books and covers Jesus's life and the work of his followers.

The reference notations in the Bible, such as Romans 3:23, are analogous to line numbers in a Shakespearean play. They serve as a study aid. Since the Bible is much longer and more complex than a play, its reference notations are more involved.

As already mentioned, the Bible is an amalgam of books, or sections, such as Genesis, Psalms, John, Acts, or 1 Peter. These are the names given to them, over time, based on the piece's author, audience, or purpose.

In the 1200s, each book was divided into chapters, such as Acts 2 or Psalm 23. In the 1500s, the chapters were further subdivided into verses, such as John 3:16. Let's use this as an example.

The name of the book (John) is first, followed by the chapter number (3), a colon, and then the verse number (16). Sometimes called a chapter-verse reference notation, this helps people quickly find a specific text regardless of their version of the Bible.

Here's how to find a specific passage in the Bible based on its reference: Most Bibles have a table of contents, which gives the page number for the beginning of each book. Start there. Locate the book you want to read, and turn to that page number. Then page forward to find the chapter you want. Last, skim that page to find the specific verse.

If you want to read online, just pop the entire reference, such as 2 Timothy 3:16, into a search engine, and you'll get lots of links to online resources. You can also go directly to BibleGateway.com or use the YouVersion app.

Although the goal was to place these chapter and verse divisions at logical breaks, they sometimes seem arbitrary. Therefore, it's a good practice to read what precedes and follows each passage you're studying since the text before or after it may have relevant insight into the part you're exploring.

Learn more about the greatest book ever written at ABibleADay.com, which has a Bible blog, summaries of the books of the Bible, a dictionary of Bible terms, Bible reading plans, and other resources.

Acknowledgments

I sincerely thank:

God, for giving me direction, patience, and grace.

My dear wife, who doesn't complain when my writing takes me away from her.

The Kalamazoo Christian Writers critique group.

My amazing administrative assistant Shara Anjaynith Cazon.

James L. Rubart, for encouragement and advice.

Joanna Penn, my online mentor from afar, for teaching me about writing and publishing.

The many people who have helped, encouraged, and taught me over the years about writing and book publishing.

Mostly, I'm grateful for each person who reads this book. May God bless you through my ministry of words.

About Peter DeHaan

P eter DeHaan, PhD wants to change the world one word at a time. His books and blog posts discuss God, the Bible, and church, geared toward spiritual seekers and church dropouts. Many people feel church has let them down, and Peter seeks to encourage them as they search for a place to belong.

But he's not afraid to ask tough questions or make religious people squirm. He's not trying to be provocative, but he seeks truth, even if it makes some people uncomfortable. Peter urges Christians to push past the status quo and reexamine how they practice their faith in every area of their lives.

Peter DeHaan earned his doctorate, awarded with high distinction, from Trinity College of the Bible and Theological Seminary. He lives with his wife in beautiful Southwest Michigan and wrangles crossword puzzles in his spare time.

A lifelong student of the Bible, Peter wrote the 700-page website ABibleADay.com to encourage people to explore the Bible, the greatest book ever written. His popular blog, at PeterDeHaan.com, addresses biblical spirituality, often with a postmodern twist.

Connect with him on Goodreads, Twitter, Facebook, LinkedIn, Instagram, Pinterest, and YouTube, all accessible from his website, PeterDeHaan.com.

If you liked *The Friends and Foes of Jesus*, please consider leaving a review online. That would be amazing. Your reviews will help other people discover this book and encourage them to read it too.

Thank you.

Other Books by Peter DeHaan

The Bible Bios series:

- *Women of the Bible: The Victorious, the Victims, the Virtuous, and the Vicious*

The Dear Theophilus series:

- *Dear Theophilus: A 40-Day Devotional Exploring the Life of Jesus through the Gospel of Luke*
- *Dear Theophilus, Acts: 40 Devotional Insights for Today's Church*
- *Dear Theophilus, Isaiah: 40 Prophetic Insights about Jesus, Justice, and Gentiles*
- *Dear Theophilus, Minor Prophets: 40 Prophetic Teachings about Unfaithfulness, Punishment, and Hope*
- *Dear Theophilus, Job: 40 Insights About Moving from Despair to Deliverance*

The 52 Churches series:

- *52 Churches: A Yearlong Journey Encountering God, His Church, and Our Common Faith*
- *The 52 Churches Workbook: Become a Church that Matters*
- *More Than 52 Churches: The Journey Continues*
- *The More Than 52 Churches Workbook: Pursue Christian Community and Grow in Our Faith*

Other books:

- *Woodpecker Wars: Celebrating the Spirituality of Everyday Life*
- *95 Tweets: Celebrating Martin Luther in the 21st Century*
- *How Big is Your Tent? A Call for Christian Unity, Tolerance, and Love*

To be the first to hear about Peter's new books and receive updates, go to PeterDeHaan.com/updates.

Printed in Great Britain
by Amazon

75673210R00140